HYPERPOLITICS

Extreme Politicization Without Political Consequences

Anton Jäger

VERSO
London • New York

This revised English-language edition first published by Verso 2026
First published by Suhrkamp Verlag as *Hyperpolitik: Extreme Politisierung ohne politische Folgen*

The manufacturer's authorized representative in the EU for product safety (GPSR) is LOGOS EUROPE, 9 rue Nicolas Poussin, 17000, La Rochelle, France
contact@logoseurope.eu

5 7 9 10 8 6 4

Verso
UK: 6 Meard Street, London W1F 0EG
US: 207 East 32nd Street, New York, NY 10016
versobooks.com

Verso is the imprint of New Left Books

ISBN-13: 978-1-83674-207-4
ISBN-13: 978-1-83674-209-8 (US EBK)
ISBN-13: 978-1-83674-208-1 (UK EBK)

British Library Cataloguing in Publication Data
A catalogue record for this book is available from the British Library

Library of Congress Cataloging-in-Publication Data
A catalog record for this book is available from the Library of Congress

Typeset in Garamond by Biblichor Ltd, Scotland
Printed and bound by CPI Group (UK) Ltd, Croydon, CR0 4YY

ESTRAGON: I can't go on like this.
VLADIMIR: That's what you think.

—Samuel Beckett, *Waiting for Godot*

Wall Street wins every election.
Now you can, too.

—Slogan for the Kalshi election betting app

Contents

Preface: Hyperpolitics, USA

Speeding through Reagan's America for a Tocquevillian travelogue about "the only remaining primitive society on earth," Jean Baudrillard noted a paradox about US power in the late 1980s. "America no longer has the same hegemony," yet "it is, in a sense, uncontested and incontestable." Presaging the unipolar moment that would follow, he claimed that "American power does not seem inspired by any spirit or genius of its own" but rather "works by inertia." If the US originally possessed the features of power, was it now "at the face-lift stage?" Or was it rather entering a phase of hysteresis, the process by which something continues to develop by inertia, whereby an effect persists even when its cause has disappeared? For Baudrillard, this was the real crisis of American power: "a potential stabilization by inertia, of an assumption of power in a vacuum," much like "the loss of immune defenses in an overprotected organism."[1]

Baudrillard offered two explanations for said crisis. The first was the absence of dependable adversaries. The US had been more powerful in the two decades after 1945, but so too were the ideas and passions ranged against it: "There is no real opposition anymore; the combative periphery has now been reabsorbed (China, Cuba, Vietnam); the great anticapitalist ideology has been emptied of substance." The second explanation was endogenous—a loss of inner dynamism: "But here again, though it seems quite clear the American machine has suffered something like a break in the current, or a breaking of the spell, who can say whether this is the product of a depression or of a supercooling of the machinery?"[2]

Given America's political landscape in the 2020s, Baudrillard's diagnosis seems prophetic. There are enemies everywhere now—from Tehran to Moscow to Beijing; not to mention Palestine's embattled defenders in Lebanon, Yemen, Syria, and Iraq—but scant recovery of a "spirit or genius." Although America's status as a world hegemon appears nominally secure—a formal empire stretching from Okinawa to Guam via Ramstein and Incirlik; unchallenged control over the global reserve currency; the most influential culture industry and most powerful armed forces in human history—the costs of America's faltering machine have become acutely clear. The assorted patch-ups for the malaise—globalized cheap labor, bottomless household debt—began to come unstuck in 2008; the next round of fixes—quantitative easing, near-zero interest rates—fueled a housing crisis while channeling funds to tech monopolies and the super rich.

Over the past decade, the country's political scene has undergone a series of spectacular convulsions, with the two parties and electorates seeming to drift ever further apart. Despite America's unrivaled dominance on the world stage and continued cultural magnetism, Democrats and Republicans now find it nigh impossible to cohabit the same political space. In recent presidential contests, key postulates of liberal democracy—legitimate opposition, peaceful handover of power, constitutional continuity—appeared up for grabs. Extraparliamentary mobilization, on the streets and in the courts, was egged on from on high; the anti-Trump resistance matched by the Capitol rioters of January 6; the battery of legal cases against the forty-fifth president by the prosecution of the hapless son of the forty-sixth. "Stabilization by inertia" has eroded American elites' capacity to buy consent from the populace—and from each other.

Since Andrew Jackson's 1828 election in the first direct presidential vote—after which electors were allowed to hold a cookout in the Oval Office—American politics has been marked by a compound of demotics and plutocracy. In 2024, a late-modern rendition of this amalgam was delivered with flair, yet not without a tinge of paranoia absent in previous presidential cycles and clouded by a sense that the US has increasingly lost its grip on political developments at home and abroad, symbolized in a head of state whose mental capacity was now a matter of conjecture.

The 2024 election provided its own perpetuation of the turbulence. Presiding over an inflationary economy slowly cooling down and an international order bursting at the seams, Harris and Biden's Democrats sought to consolidate a transversal bloc to stabilize their grip on American power in the coming decade and put the world economy on track for a green transition. In the meantime, the GOP fully acquiesced to its Bonapartist drift: a hollowed-out party, more business cartel than mass outfit, was colonized by Trump operatives blusteringly prepping themselves for regime change. The party conventions were showcases: WWE wrestlers and country stars pledging to physically shield their candidate from harm at the RNC, Georgia rappers counting down to state announcements at the DNC; Sun Belt frat boys for Trump, Ivy League poetesses for Harris.

The social anatomy of the two parties reflects the shifting tectonics of American political economy in the 2010s, stuck between the supposed imperatives of green reindustrialization and those of on- and offshore fossil fuel production; inflation-fighting and continued demand for the dollar as the world's safest asset. Two blocs have coagulated around this complex. On the one hand, a cross-class, carbon-intensive coalition is grouped around Trump and his cronies, mostly purged of GOP neoconservative stalwarts, and trading suburban conservatives for peripheral blue-collar workers, along with rural petty bourgeois, exurban middle management, real estate capitalists, crypto merchants, Silicon Valley's right wing, and steel producers who survived the *laissez-faire* onslaught of the 1980s. By contrast to the coalition that Reagan assembled, Trump's is denuded of white college graduates but buoyed by white voters without college degrees.[3] It benefits enormously from the antimajoritarian features of the US Constitution and relies on voter suppression both formal and informal for its mandate. Its mobilizational capacity was cushioned by a Ford-like tech tycoon who until recently hoped to use Trump to guarantee his access to state funds, while some labor leaders have warmed to a newly revisionist right in the party formally interested in codetermination schemes and collective wage bargaining.

On the other side stands a broad-tent Democratic Party which seems to have redefined the very notion of an "inter-class" coalition. Sociologically, the DNC now houses urban professionals, left-liberal activists, civil rights veterans, intelligence operatives, and every faction of American capital from Palo Alto "progressives" to Wall Street *haute finance*. A visitor to the 2024 Democratic National Convention in Chicago noted that it now acts as the party of labor and of capital; the party of debtors and of bankers; the party that mocks the Ivy League but is largely run by Ivy Leaguers; the party of anti-monopolists and of Silicon Valley; the party for immigrants and for border security; the party of insiders and of the marginalized; the party of the football team and of the sorority; the party of family and of freedom; the party of ceasefires and of the war machine; the party that opposes fascism but abets a genocide.[4] That even-handedness needs correction, though: bankers and warmongers predominate in Democrat ruling circles, the indebted and the marginalized among its rank and file. Perhaps the nearest comparison would be an inverted Peronist developmental bloc, with the industrial proletariat left out and finance capital firmly in the saddle over its manufacturing counterpart.

At face value, the current American political scene offers a marked contrast to the cycles of quiescence in the 1990s and early 2000s. Then, journalistic brouhaha over sex scandals and election fraud papered over the growing retreat from public life initiated by the American populace. Turnout fell to 49 percent of the voting-age population in the presidential election of 1996. Three years later, as Clinton handed a presidential medal to John Rawls, lauding him as "perhaps the greatest political philosopher of the twentieth century" and one who had "helped a whole generation of learned Americans revive their faith in democracy," popular disengagement was reaching levels reminiscent of the early Jim Crow era and the Progressive era.[5] Now, however, workplace and community associations were dissolving in the acid of deindustrialization and triumphant market logic. Always an instantiation of imperfect party competition, the American duopoly was becoming an effective example of *non*-competition; the semi-sovereign people, as political scientist Elmer Schattschneider had once termed them, were increasingly nonsovereign.[6] In conditions of convergence, culture wars alone offered a simulacrum of rivalry.

This postpolitical quietude persisted into the early 2000s. As Perry Anderson noted in a reflection on the 2000 election, the illusion of choice between presidential contenders hid the rigidity of the consensus underlying the contest. Gore's loss of the presidency had "predictably given rise to partisan legend depicting it as an unprecedented theft of the popular will, ushering in a regime of the direst social and political consequences." Yet to Anderson there was "every reason to take a coolly skeptical view of both claims"; "the gap between Gore and Bush," after all, "was modest," while a "Left that adopted [the myth] exposed itself as a frightened dependency of the Democratic establishment," unable to think outside of the two-party norm.[7] As Anderson reiterated on the eve of Obama's election, "partisan conflict and ideological tension are now much more intense [in the US] than in Europe," not due to increased social conflict but to "America's schizophrenic value-system—a culture combining the most unbridled commercialization, with the most devout sacralization, of life: 'liberal' and 'conservative' in equal extremes," with "scarcely any relevance for opposition to capital."[8]

A short quarter-century later, some coordinates of the portrait offered by Anderson appear explicitly out of date. With the fallout from the financial crisis marking a clear turning point, protests on campuses and in the streets have seen a spectacular increase. Electoral participation rose, too. In November 2008, as Wall Street teetered on the brink, turnout reached 61.6 percent of the eligible voting-age population. In 2020 it hit 66 percent, the highest proportion of Americans to cast a vote for a presidential candidate since 1900, receding slightly in 2024 to 64 percent, the second highest in over a century.[9]

Political emotions have become not only more heated but more tenacious. Compared to the speed with which uproar over the Supreme Court's ruling for Bush Jr. on the Florida recount in 2000 subsided, supposed instances of democratic backsliding—whether from the right or the left—are now the subject of sustained indignation. Another metric of high feeling: the frequency of presidential assassination attempts this past season has already outpaced all campaigns in the last four decades. There were three in the late nineteenth century—Lincoln in 1865, Garfield in 1881, McKinley in 1901—followed some sixty years later by Kennedy and the failed shot at Reagan in 1981, the last on record until 2024. To date, two attempts have been made on Trump's life, a clear indication of the choice matrix which American citizens discern in the coming election. Polarized, paranoid, zero-sum, American political life now outstrips much of Europe in terms of voting tallies and popular involvement, as well as cultural partisanship. Consent to the American ruling order can no longer be taken for granted.

Yet in other important respects, the essentials of Anderson's analysis have stood the test of time. Both parties are still committed to preserving American hyperpower abroad, with minor inflections in modality. Varieties of marketization still characterize the political offerings: on the Democrat side, a transfer state stimulating ecological investment through subsidies and profit guarantees; and tariff walls and tax cuts for the Republicans. The term "party" is perhaps too flattering for these loose coteries of elected officials, donors, publicists, and would-be candidates, with no formal membership models and little to no civil society infrastructure, except for NGO personnel. Instead, the GOP and DNC are better understood as para-state vessels that have changed remarkably little since their description by Engels in 1891:

> Nowhere do "politicians" form a more separate, powerful section of the nation than in North America. There, each of the two great parties which alternately succeed each other in power is itself in turn controlled by people who make a business of politics . . . We find here two great gangs of political speculators, who alternately take possession of the state power

> and exploit it by the most corrupt means and for the most corrupt ends.[10]

Meanwhile, after a decade of political turmoil, levels of civic membership and associational density that characterized the era of mass politics have barely recovered from the historic nadirs to which they dropped in the 1990s. For fledgling social movements operating in debt-driven service economies, the solidarities of the online world remain an insufficient replacement for those of the local community and workplace.

Predictably, this situation has initiated a frantic round of historical analogizing by the coastal intelligentsia. To analysts, the United States is experiencing its own Weimar moment, a return to the Gilded Age, teleporting back to the early Nixon era, or reliving the Old World's Wars of Religion. Some dominant hermeneutic strands can be sifted here. Since Trump's *éclat* in 2016, a host of historians and sub-intellectuals have prophesied the country's tendential slide into fascism. Stories about terrorized Ohio residents, increased paramilitary activity and exterminationist rhetoric usually make up the argument in question, with the Proud Boys as a return of Freikorps militancy and a party cadre dedicated to Project 2025. Trumpism here presents a contemporary iteration of a far-right threat indigenous to the previous century.

The comparison lacks obvious bite on many fronts. Most of all, it suppresses one of the key elements of any far-right threat throughout the twentieth century: the presence of a left on the verge of a revolutionary breakthrough. Even in the most conventional analyses offered in the Third Period, fascism had to be understood on a dual timeline: an inability of bourgeois classes to stabilize their rule after the Great War, and an increasingly assertive proletariat vying for state power. Caught in this limbo, ruling elites invited the parties of frustrated veterans to step in to solve the deadlock by smashing the anticapitalist threat; fascism expressed both the resolution and repression of the revolutionary intermezzo. None of these features apply to the contemporary American case. What does the fascist heuristic accomplish, then? Looking back, its main consequence was to rally the disaffected left behind their lesser-evil capitalist masters—as if Biden's crimes paled to nothing beside the not-dissimilar ones of Trump.

A more telling analogy is the suggestion that the US is experiencing a "second Gilded Age."[11] Here there are some similarities to be traced. In the first Gilded Age, party polarization prevailed over an extremely unequal economy amid the Second Industrial Revolution. On reelection, Trump moved to levy "McKinley-like tariffs," hoping to protect the steel sector against global overcapacity, while a devaluation of the dollar is now indirectly being pursued. In the late nineteenth century, a populist insurgency from outside the party steered it in a different direction, seeking to loosen the money supply. Then, as now, the Democrats were seen as a predominantly inflationary coalition, in favor of decoupling from a repressive gold standard, while the Republicans stood out as a deflationary bloc bent on maintaining the nation's industrial developmental trajectory.

There the analogies also quickly end. Rather than a digital outfit with loosely coordinated actors, populism grew out of a cooperative farming movement that had already achieved a foothold across the South and Midwest; only after much delay were they co-opted by establishment Democrats. This frontier peasantry sought to launch itself into corporate modernity. The era was one of rising rather than stagnating American power; US steel production had already overtaken Britain's in the 1890s;

mass immigration was at an all-time high. The machine, as Baudrillard might have said, was just revving up.

The contemporary situation thus presents a recalcitrant hybrid, difficult to relate to historical exempla. On the one hand, popular involvement in American politics has seen a relative resurgence compared to the disengagement of the 1990s and early 2000s. On the other, institutionalized involvement is at an all-time low, while American parties have only further cartelized and fused with their media or donor classes.

Throughout the recent "decade of protest," the secular decline in American membership organizations also accelerated; unions, clubs, associations, political parties, and even—spectacularly for American life—churches lost members, exacerbated by the rise of a new digital media circuit and tightening labor laws, accelerated by the "loneliness epidemic" that metastasized out of the actual one of 2020. The result is a curiously K-shaped recovery: while the erosion of American civic life proceeds apace, the country's public sphere is increasingly subject to convulsive agitation and controversy, from online conspiracy theories to the storming of government buildings. General discontent runs high, fueling political emotions; anger at police racism or Zionist violence—at immigrant crime or Chinese weather balloons—boils over.

The result is a preponderance of social media "wars of movement" over institution-building "wars of position," with the primary forms of political engagement as fleeting as market transactions. This is more a matter of necessity than of choice: the legislative environment for durable movement building remains hostile, and American activists must contend with a vitiated social landscape and an unprecedentedly expansive culture industry.

~

Beneath such structural constraints lie questions of strategy. While the internet has radically lowered the costs of political expression, it has also pulverized the terrain of radical politics, blurring the borders between party and society and spawning a chaos of vaguely mandated online actors. What Hobsbawm called "collective bargaining by riot" remains preferable to postpolitical apathy.[12] Yet without formalized membership parties, American protest politics is unlikely to return us to the superpolitical 1930s. Instead, it may usher in postmodern renditions of *ancien régime* peasant uprisings: oscillations between passivity and activity trailing presidential media cycles, without ever reducing the overall power differential within society. Hence the divergent recovery typical of the 2020s, distinct from the late twentieth-century landscapes surveyed by Anderson and Baudrillard.

The long decade of protest that started after the 2008 credit crash can then be recast less as a successful assault on the Washington citadel from below than as a mutation in the methods of managing elite-mass relations. The solution to the 2008 crisis of massively overleveraged financial institutions—pumping the stock exchange and asset prices—further widened the gap between top and base across American politics, as it did between capital fractions. Yet it has not tilted the social gradient, and popular oversight over the apparatus of government remains weak.

This is the checkerboard on which the new political surge has been playing out. The world hegemon's public sphere has been reoccupied, yet the burst of repoliticization has not increased popular control over government, nor has it put important areas of policymaking within grasp. The spectacular mismatch between input and output, which American political scientists had long diagnosed—public support for a proposal (for instance, Medicare) being negatively correlated with its chance of being implemented as a policy—has only deepened, as the Biden-Harris record shows.[13]

Heaping money on America's misfiring machine—$8 trillion under Trump I, another $6 trillion under Biden—combined with proxy wars and reshoring ("a foreign policy for the middle class"), produced a hectic spurt that saw real wages fall far behind prices for food, fuel, and housing, the gains in headline GDP growth going disproportionately to the top 20 percent. Two-thirds of American households reported living paycheck to paycheck, while 57 percent found the higher borrowing costs under Biden especially hard.[14]

Behind the current conjuncture lurk questions which American left-wing thinkers were keener to tackle in the 2010s, when debates about surrogate parties, dirty breaks, or left-wing caucuses maintained a constant relevance. Today, very few of these still stand on the mental radar of the left. As Tim Barker has noted, leading figures in American progressivism have maintained a highly Oedipal relationship to the Democrats. On the one hand, it is the party somehow uniquely responsible for a resolution to Israel's genocidal punishment campaign, and on the other, it has long served as a hallowed institution of elite Zionism and the Cold War security state.[15] Ironically, the result of the extraparty assault of the 2010s has been to tighten the hold of the DNC as the horizon of the American left. Heightened political emotions can also be captured by party cartels.[16] After a decade of experimentation with semi-independent party activity, a Squad that still sees itself as an anxious battalion for a better Democratic Party is the main remnant of America's left-populist wave.

The upshot is not necessarily dysfunctional for the country's ruling order. What it presages for the immediate future is probably more of the same: extraparliamentary challenges, legal contestation, high political emotion—and, just as under Biden, the promulgation of a bipartisan agenda that can pass a gridlocked

Congress. Internationally, this means material support and legal cover for Israeli expansionism and a proxy war on Iran, as well as an aggressive stance toward China and a proxy war with Russia, both maintained with a roughly bipartisan degree of ambivalence. Domestically, it suggests an ongoing aggressive-permissive policy on the southern border of the US, continued tensions around state-governed abortion policies, further tweaks to the tax code, and a recurrent bait-and-switch on tariffs. Hysteresis *à la* Baudrillard may have a long way yet to run.

Wolfgang Tillmans, *Love (Hands in Hair)* (1989)

I

A Grin Without a Cat

The photographs come in a bright, nearly fluorescent hue. Their connecting theme is "love." In a portrait called *Love (Hands in Hair)*, for instance, a woman with reddish hair is clutched by a pair of male hands reaching from outside the frame. In *Love (Hands Praying)*, a woman with eyes shut meditates in the anonymity of the nightclub. The people in the photographs dance to music modeled on noises emitted by the industrial machinery of Detroit and Manchester, the twin birth cities of techno.

By 1989, however—the year in which these photos were taken—the factories had fallen silent. Many had been dismantled, some relocated abroad. Traveling through a Chinese megacity some years later, the German photographer Hilla Becher noticed a reassembled copy of a steel mill she had once shot in Europe.[1] The youngsters photographed by Wolfgang Tillmans seek to dance away industry, politics, history itself.

It is worth noting the time and place of Tillmans's shots. They document Thatcherite London and Berlin at the moment the Wall is crumbling. To the east, state socialism is nearing collapse. A rigorously global capitalism is ascendant. The same year that Francis Fukuyama announces the "end of history," Tillmans's camera records a deliberate exercise in collective amnesia: an attempt to exorcise the ideological specters of the last century. As Tillmans recalls in an interview:

> That's how living together could be: being peaceful together and enjoying the senses. It seemed a very tangible and inherently political thing to me . . . Suddenly everybody felt that there was this utopia that was very real, and you could actually live this utopian dream.[2]

The photographer's testimony evokes a mood palpable across the OECD world. In a foreword to the 1992 reissue of his *Society of the Spectacle*, French philosopher Guy Debord anticipated a planet "officially unified" as "a single bloc in the consensual organization of the global market."[3] Two years later, the Communist Party of Italy's erstwhile leader Achille Occhetto traveled to Wall Street, declaring its banks "the temple of civilization"; NATO headquarters in Brussels, he ventured, was "the center of world peace."[4] Politics, an American historian observed of the 1990s, "seemed so satisfactory that the country could occupy itself with the pressing issue of whether the apparent genital pleasuring of its president by a White House intern constituted 'sex' or not."[5]

By the close of the 2010s, Tillmans's world looked disturbingly different. He had begun to photograph Black Lives Matter protests and refugee camps. His Instagram page filled with European flags and snippets of protest speeches—gray, monochrome images, quite unlike the motley palette of his *Love* series. Tillmans even became involved in mainstream politics, designing a series of posters in 2016 for the campaign to safeguard the United Kingdom's membership in the European Union. "No man is an island. No country by itself." "What is lost is lost forever." "It's a question of where you feel you belong. We are the European family." The slogans are set against Tillmans's heavenly backdrops, images of the sky as seen from an airplane window. From a distance they look like digital renditions of a Caspar David Friedrich painting.

The expectations of 1989 have capsized: Trump was elected president in the same year that Britain voted to exit the European Union. The landscapes Tillmans would once have seen on his flights to Manchester are being fenced off; across Europe, barriers are going up. His Remain placards could not salvage the lost world he first encountered as a teenager visiting England in the early 1980s. "As usual, of course, it didn't last," he remembers.

Tillmans can be forgiven his wistful tone. For the photographer, an overpowering nostalgia for post-history had kicked in. A utopia of forty years was fracturing, and he responded with references from the 1990s—figures of empathy, unity, love. This was "art after liberalism," as one critic put it.[6] In that regard, Tillmans proved a typical child of the postrevolutionary era. As Baudrillard noted in 1994, "human rights, dissidence, antiracism, SOS-this, SOS-that" were "soft, easy, *post coitum historicum* ideologies, 'after-the-orgy' ideologies for an easy-going generation which has known neither hard ideologies nor radical philosophies."[7] The contrast with the politically overcharged twentieth century was striking, in Baudrillard's view. The generation that came of age after the fall of the Wall had

> rediscovered altruism, conviviality, international charity, and the individual bleeding heart. Emotional outpourings, solidarity, cosmopolitan emotiveness, multi-media pathos: all soft values harshly condemned by the Nietzschean, Marxo-Freudian age . . . A new generation, that of the spoilt children of the crisis, whereas the preceding one was that of the accursed children of history.[8]

In Tillmans's images of Black Lives Matter protests and school climate strikes, Baudrillard might have recognized the same penchant for emotionalism, a longing for the "re-enchantment of the everyday," as a reporter put it.[9] Even if self-declaredly political, his art retained an air of detached aestheticism, awkwardly suspended between romanticism and militancy.

Tillmans's ambivalence also had a historical motive. A species of politics *did* return to the Western world after the 2008 credit crash, visible in phenomena from Occupy to the Tea Party, from Bernie Sanders to Trump. Here were developments that forced the artist to confront, in another critic's words, "the fragility of the political consensus on which his personal utopia depend[ed]."[10]

Yet this new era did not witness an integral rebirth of the mass politics from which the revelers of 1989 were liberated. Their parties had augured the era of postpolitics, in which private lives were separated from public affairs. After 2008, this order began to crack, assailed by diverse and often antagonistic forces. The resulting hybrid has turned out to be forbiddingly difficult to taxonomize. It is political, to be sure, but its modes uneasily complement and supersede the postpolitics of the 1990s, reuniting private and public in ways the classical age of democracy could not have expected. How should it be characterized?

Instant analysis is always perilous. Like a high-speed camera, histories of the present risk falling prey to the fluidity and indeterminacy of the situation they seek to capture, wedged between impressionistic detail and grand abstraction. It is all the more difficult when the present itself has become so diffuse. Much as the Marxist philosophy of history appeared obsolete in a post-historical age, the unfolding "polycrisis"—the neologism coined by Adam Tooze to capture this century's overlapping emergencies—is always one step ahead in its awesome abstractions: a 20 percent cut in GDP, 30 percent youth unemployment, $5 trillion in stimulus spending, 15 million jobs lost. History and politics are clearly taking place—but can we still say with confidence what "history" or "politics" means?

This essay ventures a tentative definition, through the lens of what I term "hyperpolitics." The concept is meant to make sense of what comes after the mass politics of the short twentieth century (1914–1989), the postpolitics of the "very long" 1990s (1989–2008), and the antipolitics of the 2010s. Attention will also be given to a range of adjacent political forms, from populism to technocracy to millennial socialism. None of these morphologies is exhaustive of the period in which it arose—periodization is rarely so neat—while a vast corpus of empirical studies could be marshaled to evaluate each. Only a small selection will be discussed here. Hyperpolitics denotes a tendency rather than a totalizing style. Nevertheless, this book argues that it constitutes a gravitational pole in the force field of twenty-first century politics. As such, it is indispensable for understanding the dynamics of mobilization and contestation that determine the contemporary scene. But these can only be grasped when situated in a longer history, linking past and present in an effort of patient distantiation.

Taken together, the political forms canvased in this book—mass politics, postpolitics, antipolitics, hyperpolitics—may be visualized on a Cartesian plane structured by two axes: a politicization axis, measuring degrees of mobilization, and a social axis, measuring degrees of civic affiliation and membership. Plotted on these, the first line—an aggregate of turnout, protest activity, political assassination—shows a marked uptick in the wake of the 2008 credit crunch. At the same time, this upward sloping curve is crossed by a downward-sloping line: a continuous decline of indices tracking civic engagement. Mass politics, in this schema, belongs to a world in which society is both highly socialized and politicized, populated by movements with clearly identifiable social bases and ideologies. Its year of inception can be situated somewhere between 1848 and 1914; its passing between 1973 and 1989. After a mass-political peak in the 1930s, we witness a transition from a "wild" to a more "embedded" variant after 1945, as the postwar economic boom tempers militancy and encourages a newfound emphasis on the consumer household.

Postpolitics, by comparison, speaks to a world both depoliticized and desocialized, in which citizens retreat from collective life into the private sphere. Properly inaugurated in 1989, it spans the 1990s and early 2000s, only temporarily interrupted by the wave of antiglobalization protests that ushered in the millennium.

Antipolitics and hyperpolitics develop, in turn, out of a conjuncture that is repoliticized but continues to be marked by the erosion—or even accelerated disintegration—of social bonds. The antipolitical phase begins in the wake of the Great Financial Crisis, as repoliticization starts to take hold of certain middle-class layers. Its locus classicus is the 2010s. Equal parts intensification of this trend and reaction to it, the advent of hyperpolitics can be dated to the final years of the decade.

No hard mathematical proof can be proffered for the shift from post- to anti- to hyperpolitics. Figure 1 is therefore less an exact representation of historical reality than an intuitive diagram, synthesizing fragments of existing graphs—of trade union density, incidence of political assassinations, size and frequency of demonstrations—offered by way of illustration.

In what follows, each political form under discussion is elucidated by reference to cultural objects that conjure its sensibility;

Figure 1: Politicization and institutionalization in historical development

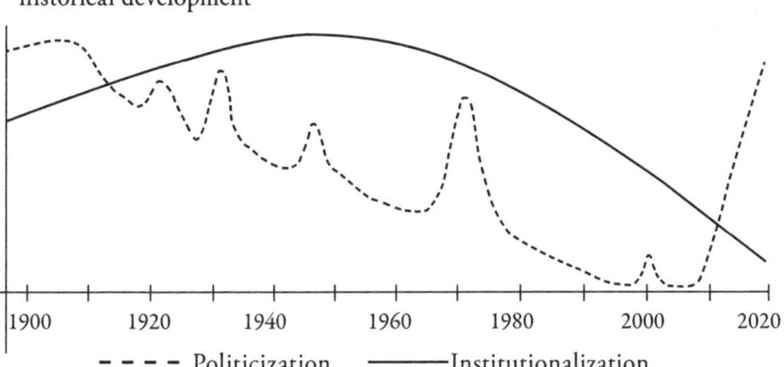

each is then placed on a parallel grid with socioeconomic coordinates. Schematically, mass politics represents the classical mode of industrial modernity; postpolitics coincides with Western deindustrialization and a new phase of globalization; antipolitics is the offspring of the chaotic management of the 2008 crisis and its aftermath. Somewhere in the middle of the 2010s, amid the Trump-Brexit moment, hyperpolitics emerges.

Hyperpolitics confronts us with a new mode of interaction between public and private. It is dynamic, intense, and polarizing, yet also ideologically diffuse, visibly modeled on the fluidity of the online world. While Jürgen Habermas sees in social media the signs of a new structural transformation of the public sphere, the 2020s have brought repoliticization under radically altered conditions. Postpolitics is indeed over, finished off by the antipolitical energies released in the 2010s. Politics once again intrudes into private life, culture, even the economy. "Today, everything is political," Adam Tooze observed in a 2023 interview. "From an American perspective, the neoliberal attempt to depoliticize the economy has failed."[11] "Almost everything about business today is political," the *Harvard Business Review* reported in 2022, and "choices that may have been clear-cut in purely economic terms . . . can now easily become complicated by politics."[12] As an American journalist confessed on the eve of the 2020 presidential election:

> I've always been interested in politics. For much of my life, this was a niche interest . . . The election of Donald Trump has made politics all consuming. Everything has become political; from what sports you watch, what products you buy, and even how you protect your own health. The people who once shared cat videos on the internet now share stridently political memes, and third-tier staffers have become celebrities.[13]

Political activity here no longer appears as the exclusive domain of specialists, technocrats, or wonks. Yet political engagement under discussion is also less exigent, more individualistic and short-term than it was for much of the twentieth century. In contrast to the "high" politics of the years 1918 to 1989, hyperpolitics is an abidingly "low" form—low-commitment, low-cost, and all too often, low-value. It thus diverges from both the postpolitics of the long 1990s and the mass politics that came before, leaving the impression of a Carrollian grin without a cat.

What was mass politics? At its height, in the immediate aftermath of the First World War, Max Weber offered a canonical definition: politics, for the German sociologist, was a "slow, strong drilling through hard boards," requiring "both passion and a sense of judgement." The person fit to take part in it had to be "a leader"—indeed, "must, in a very simple sense of the word, be a hero." "And even those who are neither of these things must," Weber intoned, "put on the armor of that steadfastness of heart which can withstand even the defeat of all hopes."[14]

Delivered in the revolutionary winter of 1919, Weber's lecture was anything but a radical manifesto. Instead, his remarks can be read as a veiled critique of the revolutionary impatience of the German Communists, who sought to imitate their Russian counterparts and "paint Germany red." Weber's audience—students from a nationalist fraternity—may have aspired to careers in the state bureaucracy. For the moment, they were being groomed to quash the country's revolution and secure the propertied order alongside right-wing Freikorps.

Despite his hostility toward the radical left, however, Weber and his opponents remained children of the same age—however hieratic, his plea for vocational intransigence reflected a form of politics that presupposed institutional involvement of the populace. Both Weber and his ideological adversaries thereby shared a vision of political engagement that was markedly more patient and sustained than that which prevails in the twenty-first century. For German Communists and fascists, the personal may well have been political, yet it would not have occurred to them to reduce the latter to the former, and they inhabited a social landscape much deeper and more expansive than the brittle societies in which we live today. The mass politics of Weber's time was certainly no less heated than our hyperpolitical moment, yet it was more solidly institutionalized.

A glance at a few contemporary case studies gives a sense of the gulf separating past from present. The protests following the killing of George Floyd mobilized millions—only to ebb just as swiftly. In 1963, participants in Martin Luther King's March on Washington wore union pins and city badges on their jackets. Among Black Lives Matter demonstrators, by contrast, few preexisting affiliations were in evidence. The movement had no cadres, at most a handful of staffers from antiracism NGOs acting as chaperones. The *gilets jaunes* blocked French highways but have long since dispersed. In the 2010s, it briefly seemed as if pirate parties were ascendant; today they are all but forgotten. Climate strikes disrupted the school day from Sweden to East Timor and then petered out. Episodes in the culture war over "woke" themes dominate social media for a few days, or hours, before being displaced by the next scandal. Like the notoriously short cycles of financial markets and digital media, the contemporary public sphere spasmodically convulses without ever crystallizing into durable infrastructure.

Hyperpolitics would be unthinkable without a particular set of social preconditions. Sociologically, it is rooted in a society in which exit options abound and citizens find it easy to move from one institution to another. Just as employment has become more precarious in the postindustrial era, abandoning a family, a relationship, a party, or a circle of friends is a much less demanding process than it was in Weber's time. Temporally, such ease of exit produces a society in which all dimensions of life are subject to short-term logics; friendships, marriages, jobs, and political commitments are compressed into ever-shorter time frames. The changing coordinates of working life incentivize hyperpolitical behavior: employees with no hope of a permanent position are unlikely to identify strongly with their professional vocation. Even at the lower rungs of the labor market, individuals relate to their affiliations as investors at the stock exchange, allocating resources and withdrawing them once the return on investment is no longer guaranteed.

The life-worlds of the online are the primary environment for this sort of deinstitutionalized, impermanent engagement, offering repertoires of social expression that require little to no long-term obligation. Atomization and acceleration go hand in hand: people are lonelier in the new century, but also more agitated; more atomized, but also more connected; angrier, yet more disoriented.

Beyond the internet, the market itself supplies a still more powerful metaphorics for our hyperpolitical present. Hyperpolitics is, above all, an eminently market-friendly type of politics, in form as well as content. Markets offer exit options; by nature, they are focused on the short term. Trading algorithms know no future. As Hayek noted, the psychology of planning and mass politics were closely related: politicians would bide their time over decades; Soviet planners read human needs across multiple five-years plans; Mao, keenly aware of the *longue durée*, hibernated in rural exile for more than twenty years. The horizon of the market, however, is much nearer: the oscillations of the business cycle offer instant rewards to participants. Today, politicians navigate by election cycle and polling averages; citizens turn out to demonstrate for a day; influencers petition or protest with a tweet. Postpolitics may be over, but its successor would be unrecognizable to a time traveler from the early twentieth century.

Halfway through her novel *The Years* (2008), Annie Ernaux gives her readers a rearview rendering of the mid-1990s reminiscent of Tillmans's portraits:

> The rumor was going around that politics was dead. The advent of a "new world order" was declared. The end of History was nigh . . . The word "struggle" was discredited as a throwback to Marxism, become an object of ridicule. As for "defending rights," the first that came to mind were those of the consumer.[15]

Born to working-class parents in 1940, Ernaux had already become one of her country's most celebrated novelists when she was awarded the Nobel Prize in 2022. First published in French in 2008, her "collective autobiography" of postwar France hit bookstores shortly before Lehman Brothers went bust and induced a heart attack in the international financial system. The English translation came out in 2017, at the close of the populist decade.

Ernaux's work diagnosed a shuttered, claustral universe in which European citizens found refuge in privacy and seclusion. "In the humdrum routine of personal existence," she recalls, "History did not matter." Politics was relegated to the back burner. Technocrats, mostly stationed in central banks and institutions such as the IMF and the European Commission, took the reins.

A suitable idiom was devised for the new world. British Prime Minister Tony Blair claimed that opposing globalization was like opposing the changing of the seasons, while the term *Alternativlosigkeit* ("alternativelessness") settled into the German vernacular. A group of Polish poets attended the opening of the country's first McDonald's; Catholic priests consecrated a Coca Cola plant. Across the ocean, the Democratic Party chose "Macarena" as the theme song for its 1996 convention. Two years later, Pizza Hut aired a TV commercial featuring Mikhail Gorbachev. The last General Secretary of the Communist Party of the Soviet Union scurries into a branch of the fast food chain on Red Square, accompanied by his granddaughter. A heated argument breaks out at one of the tables: "Thanks to him we have political instability!" complains one customer. "It's because of him that we have freedom!" the customer's son retorts angrily. "Because of him," the mother interjects at last, "we have many things—including Pizza Hut."

The mood could undoubtedly feel liberatory. Deliverance from the ideological orthodoxies of the twentieth century provoked a sense of elation, especially for those who sought to do away with the strictures of gender and race that had underpinned "organized capitalism" after the Second World War, or dissidents who had opposed their own countries' communist dictatorships. The breach opened a realm of possibilities, exemplified in a way by Tillmans's raves.

Yet the triumph of the private also entailed a thoroughgoing subordination of the public. At some remove from Tillmans's epic of liberation, Ernaux documented the transition to postpolitics with a focused ambiguity, seeing around rather than through the new order. "Since no one represented us," she writes, "it was only fitting that we do as we pleased, so that voting became a private, emotional affair, governed by last-minute impulse." "One needed the habit and long-standing memory of 'electoral duty' to bother to go to the polling station on an April Sunday in the middle of spring vacation."[16]

Drugs and dancing looked more inviting, coupled with increasingly exuberant promises of consumption. "There was an ad that read: Money, sex, drugs—choose money," Ernaux recounts. Rave music sounded a requiem for the industrial economy, its funeral rites observed at clubs and outdoor festivals. "Everything is permitted but nothing is possible" was French philosopher Michel Clouscard's prospectus for the 1990s, while his contemporary Cornelius Castoriadis saw a "society adrift" amidst "a rising tide of insignificance."[17] The writer Sam Kriss later looked back on the postpolitical period described by Ernaux from the vantage point of a younger millennial:

> Back then, it was not normal for young people to define themselves politically. My friends were fond of making grand statements like "I'm bigger than feminism" or "Politics is for little minds." The millennial generation wasn't stereotyped as preening, moralistic, or oversensitive: we were all supposed to

> be boozy nihilists, uni lads or frat bros. Back then, the problem with the voting public wasn't misinformation, or extremism, or that we were all at each other's throats—it was that we couldn't even be bothered to vote.[18]

Two decades of political turmoil later, these testimonies feel at once familiar and strange, like one of Magritte's domestic interiors. The individualization and the decline of collective institutions they registered have not been halted. Aside from a few outliers, political parties have not regained their members. Churches have not refilled their pews. Unions have not been organizationally resurrected. Electoral competition is still highly constrained, driven by a narrow cartel of career politicians and specialists ever at the mercy of hostile markets. Across the West, civil society remains mired in a deep and protracted crisis, with political action monopolized by NGOs, online personas, entrepreneurs, and philanthropists. At least in one abiding sense, this chapter of the postpolitical saga is not closed.

Yet some coordinates have undeniably shifted. For one, the cocktail of diffidence, euphoria, and apathy characteristic of Tillmans's and Ernaux's 1990s, the heavy post-historic affect visible in their novels and photographs, barely applies today. Triviality and excitement—the "depressive hedonism" that British writer Mark Fisher famously diagnosed in the early 2000s—have morphed into something altogether more recondite.[19] President Joe Biden was elected in 2020 by a record turnout of 81 million. Four years later his opponent garnered 77 million votes. The Brexit referendum was the largest democratic vote in Britain's history. The global Black Lives Matter movement won mass acclamation—on its call, many of the world's biggest corporations and celebrities took up the mantle of racial justice, from Jeff Bezos redrawing the Amazon logo to David

Guetta sampling Martin Luther King speeches during a rooftop DJ set.

The George Floyd protests were the most numerous in American history—thousands of demonstrations, with an estimated attendance of up to 26 million. In the summer of 2020, almost one-tenth of the American adult population took to the streets, with corporate lawyers and unemployed teenagers rioting into the early hours of the morning. Today, platforms like TikTok, YouTube, and X overflow with political content, from vloggers reciting anarchist pamphlets to right-wing influencers raving about refugees. Scolds and advice columnists ponder the ethics of personal consumption, from veganism to climate budgeting. Self-help manuals advise citizens to detect and exorcise their racial biases.

The notion of hyperpolitics has another claim to paternity. In 1993, the philosopher Peter Sloterdijk published a short book titled *Im selben Boot: Versuch über die Hyperpolitik* (In the Same Boat: An Essay on Hyperpolitics). Sloterdijk focused on a dimension of politics that political scientists typically label "polity," denoting the general structure and composition of a political community. His particular interest lay in what he called "fantasies of togetherness" and "the reality-illusions that give rise to societies."[20] Via a sequence of maritime metaphors, he sketched a three-stage theory of human history, beginning with a "paleo-political" period, pictured as an argosy of rafts "on which small groups of people drift through vast spaces of time" without forming more definite projects or entering into contact with other human groups.[21] With the dawn of the Axial Age came the epoch of "state galleys and imperial frigates": advanced civilizations, great empires, and "classical politics." Here, "state athletes"—pharaohs, Caesars, senators—were tasked with "uniting a thousand, ten thousand, a hundred thousand hordes . . . in such a way that collective efforts could be demanded of them, to construct irrigation projects, fight crusades, and pay tributary taxes."[22]

Industrialization and increasing global interconnection gave rise to a wholly new structure, in Sloterdijk's account: the "hypersphere." The distinction between rulers and ruled began to blur; "people on the street" now preoccupied themselves with questions that were once the preserve of foreign ministers; social cohesion became increasingly difficult to sustain, to the point that no one really believed "that this society is theirs." Politicians, Sloterdijk claimed, rarely proved equal to the "challenges of the new condition," hence "the growing mass unease with the political class."[23] The "journey into contemporary hyperpolitics," he argued, was experienced by many "as a high-speed train ride into an empire of confusion." Politics similarly came to resemble "a chronic near-miss mass-collision on a foggy motorway."[24] Sloterdijk's preferred metaphor for this final stage was an image of "super-ferries, so vast as to be almost unsteerable, plowing through a sea of drowning people, with waves battering the hull and anxious conferences unfolding onboard."[25]

As Sloterdijk notes at the end of this philosophical *tour de force*, "when Western men and women style themselves as 'democrats' today, they do not do so out of any pretense of contributing to the public good, but because they rightly regard democracy as the type of society that allows them *not* to think about the state and the art of belonging together." For Sloterdijk, sociologists were correct to suspect that the individualism spreading across the West in the 1980s and 1990s constituted

> a new wave of insulation, one that goes well beyond the familiar standards of individuation in old Europe. Increasingly, people are sealing themselves off not just from institutions or parties, but from *society as such* . . . A growing multitude of

> loosely connected individuals drift, propelled by the inner logic of industrial life, into a second-order solitude among their peers . . . a solitude for which the usual moralizing labels like "apolitical" or "antisocial" do not apply.[26]

"The single-occupancy apartment," Sloterdijk concluded, "is the vanishing point of civilization, and living alone the crowning achievement of a millennia-long process of anthropological refinement."[27]

In May 2020, the radio station *France Inter* commissioned a series of prominent writers to reflect on the consequences of the pandemic. One of the first invitees was Michel Houellebecq, reporting on the home front while holed up in his Paris apartment. The tenor of most other interventions was one of hopeful transition, painting COVID as a civilizational watershed, leaving behind a world remade. Houellebecq disagreed violently: "After lockdown we will not wake up in a new world; it will be the same as before, just a bit worse." COVID was "a banal virus, unglamorously related to some obscure flu-like illnesses, with poorly understood survival conditions, unclear characteristics—sometimes benign, sometimes deadly, not even sexually transmissible: in short, a virus without qualities."[28]

Houellebecq has long figured as the emblematic novelist of the postpolitical era. His debut, *Extension du domaine de la lutte* (1994)—*Whatever*, in English translation—encapsulates the nihilism of a generation that has known neither politics nor history and simply chases instant gratification. *The Elementary Particles* (1998) likewise chronicles the hedonistic 1990s, this time enriched by the latest developments in space travel and genetic engineering. *Lanzarote* (2000), a shorter prose piece, addresses the theme of touristification.

As the American critic Christopher Caldwell has pointed out, the age of postpolitics "require[d] dismantling hierarchies, institutions and cultures." Although presented as an economic imperative, this generated a nettlesome problem for fiction writers, since the "same hierarchies, institutions, and culture are what novels have always been about," even if society "does not nurture these the way it did in an age of large and loyal families, intertangled commercial enterprises and long-settled communities." In Caldwell's view, Houellebecq "faced this predicament with artistic integrity, refusing to fantasize that individuals in our time can somehow be re-inserted into such 'novelistic' webs of meaning."[29]

By the time of *Platform* (2001), however, the party is already nearing its end, and an inescapable atmosphere of paranoia has kicked in—Islamic terrorists attack a Thai beach resort the dreamy Westerners have built for themselves. In *Submission* (2015), the hitherto peripheral threat turns into a frontal assault when Islamists take over the French state and found a caliphate on the Seine. We have awakened from our postpolitical reverie, but the alternative that Houellebecq imagines is a regressive traditionalism with no popular appeal, workable only through blackmail and open coercion. Antipolitics cannot fulfil the expectations it generates. In *Serotonin* (2019), a rival option surfaces: the disorganized, evanescent occupation of crossings and motorways, farmers blocking the highway and opening fire on the French police. In a Nostradamus-like aperçu, Houellebecq presages the Yellow Vest protests that broke out only a few months before the novel's release, in response to a fuel tax hike announced by President Emmanuel Macron.

Lately, however, the novelist appears to be losing his grip. In his most recent book, *Annihilation* (2022), the plot at first appears eminently contemporaneous. Set in 2026, its protagonist Paul Raison is an advisor to his friend Bruno Juge, France's minister of economy and finance. Presidential elections are underway, and Juge is planning to run. Suddenly, videos begin circulating online depicting the minister's beheading, shot in the style of ISIS propaganda and made with such ingenuity that IT specialists are at pains to figure out who composed the clips. A series of mysterious cyberattacks occurs, shutting down traffic in several international ports.

At this point, the novel changes gear. Paul leaves Paris to visit his father, on life support after suffering a stroke. The homecoming involves his sister Cécile, a loyal Le Pen voter and born-again Catholic, now married to an unemployed notary. We also get glimpses of Paul's mother Suzanne, a conservationist, and his brother Aurélien, an archivist at the Ministry of Culture in an unhappy marriage. The book ends with Paul's own descent into purgatory after a cancer diagnosis.

To the habitual *houellebecquien*, the constitutive elements of *Annihilation* will feel familiar. But there is an unmistakable sense of diminution. The novel reads as if it were written compulsively and in haste, and the tone is uncharacteristically mellow. What has happened? The central subject of Houellebecq's most original novels—the nihilistic societies of the 1990s and 2000s—has become less reliable as a target. As a raw capitalist reflex, neoliberal policies will doubtless retain their attraction. But they are hardly election winners anymore. The political culture of the 1990s has also mutated—what to do when the "entrepreneurs of the self" of the 1990s become the "zombie Catholics" of today? As Caldwell would put it, the great portraitist of the postpolitical subject has lost his model; in the resulting confusion, the natural pivot is to existentialist cliché: death, faith, Jacob wrestling with the angel, love eternal. The difficulty is symptomatic of a wider atmospheric shift. In Houellebecq's best books, the bleakness of French life—fusing personal despair and social decomposition—implicitly justified almost any form of anti-establishment revolt. Though he never explicitly endorsed the Yellow Vests, his novels largely aligned with their critique.

The characters in *Annihilation* no longer appear as the resigned victims of neoliberal restructuring. Rather, we see men and women outside of history, facing a godless universe as Christians without a church. The sister's Catholicism, for instance, is purely performative, detached from any concrete denominational infrastructure. Houellebecq may reference nearly every contemporary political orientation, from right-identitarians to anarcho-primitivists and deep ecologists, but they figure merely as unwitting agents of a "gigantic collapse," a natural disaster personified by Paul's father's comatose state.

Houellebecq anticipated two potential successors to post-politics: reactionary pseudo-traditionalism and populist rebellion, a politics of antipolitics. But he failed to predict what has shown itself to be the most consequential. Hyperpolitics promises the re-enchantment of public life for the very subjects that Houellebecq imagined had permanently withdrawn from it. In its fusion of privatized self-expression and political enthusiasm, hyperpolitics addresses the longing for purpose so characteristic of the last century, left unsatisfied since the 1990s.

In early 2022, Houellebecq announced that *Annihilation* would be his final novel. The culmination of postpolitics thus coincided with the completion of an oeuvre. This invites a retrospective on the era he immortalized in his books, one that is fast receding in the rearview mirror. With its passing, the ground gave way under Houellebecq just as it did for Tillmans. We find ourselves in a world unkind to nostalgists and futurists alike.

2

Putnam from the Left

In 2021, the Survey Center on American Life published a study of friendship patterns in the United States. Packed into ten detailed pages, the report made for disheartening reading. Identifying what they called a "friendship recession," researchers noted that Americans are increasingly lonely and isolated: 12 percent said that they did not have close friendships, compared to 3 percent in 1990, while nearly half claimed to have lost contact with friends during the COVID pandemic.[1] The psychosomatic fallout was dire: heart disease, sleep disruptions, increased risk of Alzheimer's. Together with falling marriage rates and rising virginity among American males, the friendship recession harbored potentially lethal effects; "given these extraordinary costs," the US surgeon general warned in 2023, "rebuilding social connection must be a top public health priority for our nation."[2]

A report by the EU Commission documented similar patterns: whereas 12 percent of EU citizens reported feeling lonely "more than half of the time" prior to the pandemic, the figure doubled to 25 percent in the first half of 2020, with young people between the ages of eighteen and twenty-five especially affected.[3] The studies offer a window onto a process that has overtaken many OECD countries in recent decades. As the quintessential voluntary association, friendship circles are a microcosm of other social institutions—parties, sport clubs, membership organizations, guilds.

French philosopher Jean-Claude Michéa was born in 1950 to a family of committed Communists; his mother was a typist, his father a cycling reporter for a Party newspaper. In an interview, Michéa recalled that one of the most disconcerting moments of his childhood was the day he discovered there were neighbors in the village who were not card-carrying French Communist Party (PCF) members. "That seemed unimaginable," he said, as if those people "lived outside the bounds of society itself."[4] Not coincidentally, the Parisian students of May 1968 regularly compared the Communist Party to the Catholic Church. Christians yearned for God, workers for revolution. Instead, as Christian Jambet and Guy Lardreau put it, "the Christians got the Church, and the working class got the Party."[5] For Michéa, the Party served as an extension of family, of friendship circles, of the neighborhood. Its boundaries were the boundaries of his world.

Unsurprisingly, as the once-proud PCF shriveled, social atomization swelled in Michéa's native France. "Occasionally I found myself wondering whether I'd ever see my parents again before they died," the protagonist in Houellebecq's *Submission* recollects, "but the answer was always negative, and I didn't think even a civil war could bring us together."[6] Long before the lockdowns of 2020 and 2021, Western societies had already commenced social distancing in a softer, less openly coordinated manner.

To social scientists, this refrain will sound familiar. It is the stock-in-trade of one of the classics of early twenty-first-century political science, Robert Putnam's *Bowling Alone: The Collapse and Revival of American Community* (2000). Alongside Putnam's work on Italian civil society in the 1990s, the book helped entrench the notion that civic mores in the West were eroding, and that policymakers would need to make a concerted effort to counteract said trend. *Bowling Alone* thereby served as an unofficial manifesto for a new communitarian creed, intended to soften the pitiless liberalism that had triumphed after 1989.

Putnam's argument opened with its titular observation. More and more Americans took up bowling toward the end of the twentieth century, but they increasingly undertook this activity *alone*. The sharp decline of bowling leagues was the clearest symptom.[7] Where once these had involved regular evenings and tightly knit groups with their own rituals and rules, leagues were now shutting down. The drop-off was by no means limited to alley leaderboards. Churches, trade unions, shooting clubs, and Masonic lodges all saw membership contract dramatically in the 1980s and 1990s. When the remaining members left or died, these associations began to disband. They left behind a wasteland of sociability, visible in the dilapidated *case del popolo* in Italian city centers and abandoned workingmen's clubs on the Liverpool docks. Previously, proletarians could play cards, watch a movie, or listen to a lecture in these establishments; now, these "third places"—designed neither for work nor for consumption, as Putnam would have it—lay vacant.

Putnam surveyed a variety of causes for this *grand désengagement*.[8] In the United States, middle-class families' flight to the suburbs, beginning in the 1960s, left many in neighborhoods exclusively designed for motorists, without footpaths. Consumption was democratized in the postwar boom. People spent more time in their cars, a mobile privatization of public space. Corner stores were bulldozed to make way for shopping malls, and commuter rail infrastructure lost out to highways. The steady entry of women into the labor market deprived voluntary associations of a central base of support. Employees began working longer hours than their parents had and found little time for volunteering. Television locked citizens at home in the evening—the tombstone of postwar loneliness.

Bowling Alone also ably debunked some stubborn misconceptions, starting with the idea that the welfare state was the real culprit for the civic crisis. According to this argument, "big government" in Washington had gradually usurped many of the social functions once performed by communities or individual citizens, thereby displacing local networks and private initiative. Putnam was skeptical, noting that levels of social capital were higher in Scandinavian countries than in the US, despite their far more expansive social provisions.[9] Another "controversial" interpretation, in Putnam's words, hinged on the question of race. Since the beginning of the decline in civic engagement in the 1960s coincided with the zenith of the civil rights movement, some were quick to attribute the decline to racial prejudice. White Americans, it was held, had withdrawn from clubs and associations after the end of formal segregation. But here too, data did not support the claim. Black Americans, Putnam observed, had also retreated from communal life, all while interracial enmity was declining.[10] Something more uncanny was afoot.

To illustrate his findings, Putnam compiled a pie chart weighing the various causal factors.[11] He acknowledged that the percentages were "guesstimated," based as much on intuition as on a reading of the relevant literature. Time pressure and changing work patterns accounted for, at most, 10 percent of the decline in civic activity, suburbanization explained another 10 percent; electronic entertainment media—especially television—25 percent. But the single most important factor, responsible for 50 percent, was generational change: younger cohorts were simply less engaged than their parents and grandparents. The final 5 percent of the chart was left blank, labeled "Other?"

Putnam had little use for panaceas. In 2000, he predicted that the internet would offer an uncertain substitute for older affiliations, perhaps even reinforce antisocial tendencies. "Could new 'virtual communities' simply be replacing the old-fashioned physical communities in which our parents lived?" he wondered, anticipating that online interaction would "not *automatically* offset the decline in more conventional forms of social capital." Nonetheless, it would be "hard to imagine solving our contemporary civic dilemmas without computer-mediated communication."[12] In 2020, however, the social scientist—holed up alone in his New Hampshire home during the pandemic—took a much gloomier view of the subject. In a characteristically downbeat afterword to a new edition of *Bowling Alone*, Putnam found that there was no "correlation between internet usage and civic engagement," while the future promised "cyberbalkanization" not "digital democracy." The stocks of social capital had not been replenished.[13]

Weaknesses in Putnam's approach were easy to detect by the early 2000s. For one, *Bowling Alone* spent too little time investigating the structural transformation of civil society—the rise of NGOs as substitutes for mass-membership organizations, the proliferation of evangelical megachurches and schools, especially in the United States and Brazil, and the evolution of a newly "social" internet after the dotcom crash of 2001. Another objection targeted Putnam's somewhat dubious notion of "social capital." This was meant to denote the number of contacts and networks to which an individual has access, from friendship circles to organizational memberships. But why should these qualify as "capital," an asset capable of generating returns? In this respect, at least, the book spoke to the market-friendly sensibilities of the late 1990s. Civic ties were conceived of less as an expression of collective power than as resources for individual social mobility. Relationships and community involvement might adorn college applications and help postgrads land internships; they were not going to provide the basis for any radical transformation of the social order itself.

Communitarianism and neoliberalism thereby entered an uneasy alliance in Putnam's vision. As an already meagre American welfare state was dismantled or commercialized by successive presidential administrations, families and neighborhood groups were promoted as private social safety nets. The AIDS crisis of the 1990s, for instance, was not met with an expansion of healthcare provision; in fact, many American gay men lost insurance coverage as their sexual orientation came to be considered an "uninsurable risk."[14] At the same time, banks discovered in this same demographic a new credit market, from which they had previously been excluded. Efforts to legalize same-sex marriage also gathered steam, allowing gay couples with the means to do so to set aside savings in the event of an emergency. It offered a textbook case of what Nancy Fraser would later term "progressive neoliberalism," albeit with a faintly conservative inflection.[15]

Such economism also helps explain a blind spot in *Bowling Alone*—the steep drop in union strength at the close of the century, and the corresponding slump of left-wing parties. Although Putnam addresses the world of work in passing—he mentions Reagan's crushing of the PATCO air-traffic controllers' strike in 1981, and dilapidated factory towns further west—he showed scant interest in the loss of revolutionary potential associated with the decline of trade unions, let alone the link between the stagnation of capitalist accumulation after the oil price shock of 1973 and the concomitant crisis of civil society. In a book of more than 500 pages, readers find no index entries for "deindustrialization," "capitalism," or "neoliberalism." In their place, a diffuse "globalization" is invoked as *primum movens*; the possibility that capital—with a capital *C*—may have actively undermined social capital does not qualify as a plausible hypothesis. *Bowling Alone* was meant to be the kind of book that a progressive presidential candidate might carry on the campaign trail. It was never intended as a manual for revolution.

Despite its shortcomings, Putnam's book has stood the test of time—its central insight remains valid. Midway through the 2020s, membership in secular organizations continues to decline. In Germany, for instance, the main trade union federation represented nearly 12 million workers in 1991; thirty years later, that figure had shriveled to just 5.7 million. Although public support for unions has risen in the United States, the unionization rate reached a historic low of 10.1 percent in 2021, following a brief uptick during the pandemic. In the early 1980s it still hovered around 20 percent—a sign that the renewed organizing efforts of the 2010s have not kept pace with the growth of the labor force.

While workers in certain sectors have become more militant, the Great Resignation—the wave of job quitting that swept through the tight US labor market in particular in 2021—did not lead to a direct collective assertion of worker power. Instead, as sociologist Daniel Zamora puts it, this gave rise to a politics of individual *exit*.[16] Thanks in part to government support, many workers left their jobs during and after COVID, searching for higher pay and a better work-life balance. But demands for workplace democracy and control over the production process, still commonplace in the 1970s, barely surfaced. "Workers have gained leverage and, in many sectors, wages are going up," Zamora writes, "but this is not the outcome of increased labour unrest or the demands of unions," even as "inflation is now determined by the actions of central banks rather than through collective bargaining."

The great withdrawal has also continued apace in the religious sphere. According to a Pew Research study, in 2021 a record 29 percent of Americans defined themselves as "nones," or non-religious, compared to 16 percent in 2007.[17] In the UK, attendance at Church of England services fell by around 20 percent between 2009 and 2019, before plummeting during the pandemic.[18] In Italy, the number of people attending church at least once a week declined from 18.4 million in 2006 to less than 10 million in 2023.[19]

Electoral patterns offer another acute illustration of this trend. Although turnout has been on the upswing in the past three US presidential elections, Americans now tend to vote alone.[20] Whereas they once arrived at polling stations as members of a specific party or civic group, they now enter the voting booth as individual citizens, guided by purely personal preferences—if they haven't already cast their ballots by mail.

The qualifications entered above suggest a materialist variation on Putnam's story, focused squarely on the core institutions of the mass-political era, parties and trade unions. To be sure, the latter's decline involved both push and pull factors. In Anglo-Saxon countries, in particular, antilabor legislation and employers' concerted strategies of union busting contributed to undermining the labor movement. Across much of Europe, too, laws impeded the establishment of works councils and worker representation on corporate boards, the practice known as "codetermination." Faced with globalization and deindustrialization, unions found themselves increasingly on the defensive. Meanwhile, passive alternatives to union or party power—cheap credit, self-help gospels, cryptocurrency, online forums—steadily multiplied.

In the 2010s, Putnam's digital skepticism received further confirmation. Netflix, drugs, and delivery services have turned the twenty-first-century home into a self-enclosed repository of creature comforts. "Sitting at home alone has become a lot less boring," the journalist Matthew Yglesias wrote on his blog, appropriately titled *Slow Boring*, while the ability to "stream alone" has driven up the "opportunity costs" of other activities. From a Marxist perspective, the constant refinement of personal consumption, like the attenuation of civil society, appeared as an imperative of capital itself. Collective life had to be thinned out to clear new inroads for the market.

By way of historical contrast, it is worth recalling just how dense and developed the centers of that collective life once were. In their classic sociology of unemployment in interwar Austria, Marie Jahoda, Paul Lazarsfeld, and Hans Zeisel begin by listing the many associations that existed in their "industrial village," Marienthal, a Rhenish hamlet hit hard by the Great Depression:

> A few years ago, the members of the Social Democratic Party built a workmen's clubhouse during their spare time. Marienthal has always been politically active; there has long been a great number of organizations and institutions run by the different political parties. On the Social Democratic side are the party organization, a trade union with an affiliated theatre club, the child welfare committee called Children's Friends, the Society of Free Thinkers, The Flame (a cremation society), a cycling club, the Workers' Radio Club, the Workers' Athletic Club, the Wrestling Club, the Young Socialist Workers, the Republican Home Guard, the Workers' Library, the Rabbit Breeders' Association, and the Allotment Owners' Association.[21]

The Hungarian philosopher Gáspár Miklós Tamás emphasized the political weight of such organizations. They constituted

> a counter-power of working-class trade unions and parties, with their own savings banks, health and pension funds, newspapers, extramural popular academies, workingmen's clubs, libraries, choirs, brass bands, *engagé* intellectuals, songs, novels, philosophical treatises, learned journals, pamphlets, well-entrenched local governments, temperance societies—all with their own mores, manners and style.[22]

Antonio Gramsci, writing in 1931, famously described the party as the equivalent of Machiavelli's prince:

> The modern prince, the myth-prince, cannot be a real person, a concrete individual. It can only be an organism, a complex element of society in which a collective will, which has already been recognized and has to some extent asserted itself in action, begins to take concrete form. History has already provided this organism, and it is the political party—the first cell in which there come together germs of a collective will tending to become universal and total.[23]

For an arch-conservative jurist such as Carl Schmitt, this world of organizational politics was already a source of alarm in the 1930s. In a lecture from November 1932, he complained to a group of German employers:

> We do not have a total state but a plurality of total parties. Each party realizes in itself the totality, totally absorbing their members, guiding individuals from cradle to grave, from kindergarten to burial and cremation, situating itself totally in the most diverse social groups and passing on to its membership the correct views, the correct ideology, the correct form of state, the correct economic system, and the correct

> sociability on account of the party. Old liberal-styled parties, which are not capable of such organization, are in danger of being pulverized by the millstones of the modern total party.[24]

These reflections by Gramsci and Schmitt were separated by months. Together, they mark the apogee of the "wild" mass politics of the 1930s. Notwithstanding Schmitt's protestations, the party structures he identified expanded even further in the immediate postwar years, to the extent that contemporaries spoke of "organized democracies." In Belgium and the Netherlands, separate Catholic, Protestant, socialist, and liberal milieus each had their own newspapers, youth clubs, even hospitals known as "pillars," or *zuilen*. These institutions acted as fortified bastions, mediating the relationship between individuals and the state and enabling the population to exert a measure of influence over its government.

This party democracy should not be taken for an academic abstraction. In his memoir *Returning to Reims* (2009), Didier Eribon recounts growing up in a Communist family in northeastern France. As a gay man born in 1953, Eribon always felt out of place in the universe of his working-class parents, for whom same-sex love was an expression of "bourgeois deviancy" and immigrants from Muslim countries were regularly held in contempt. The Party kept a watchful eye on militants' private as well as public lives.

Yet this hardly diminished Eribon's appreciation for the sense of social belonging the PCF had provided for his mother and father. Their membership card meant more than material advantages (though it offered those, too). As a symbol, it stood for total, immersive belonging to a community and a way of life. In a society hostile to their interests, emotions, and habits, the Party supplied cohesion and a stable sense of self. It was, Eribon wrote, "the organizing principle and the uncontested horizon of our relation to politics."[25]

> The words "the Left" really meant something important. People wanted to defend their own interests, to make their voices heard, and the way to achieve that—aside from strikes or protests—was to delegate, to hand oneself over to the "representatives of the working class" and to political leaders whose decisions were thus implicitly accepted and whose discourses you learned and repeated.[26]

This required a transfer of agency but guaranteed in return a modicum of collective power. Unlike the monads that people our public sphere, an arena for individual self-expression in which representative institutions appear intrinsically suspect, Eribon's parents became political subjects by putting themselves "into the hands of the party spokespersons, through whom workers, the 'working class,' came to exist as an organized group, as a class that was aware of itself as such." The very "way of thinking about oneself, the values one espoused, the attitudes one adopted were all to a large extent shaped by the conception of the world that the 'Party' helped to inculcate in people's minds and to diffuse throughout the social body."

Representation also fed back into political culture. In Eribon's view, party membership gradually displaced many of the prejudices that workers had absorbed from French society at large. "By means of their vote for the Communist Party," he claimed, "individuals went beyond what they were separately or serially, and the collective opinion that was produced through the mediation of the Party, which both shaped and expressed it, was in no way the reflection of the various heterogeneous opinions of any of the voters." Racist attitudes did not disappear in his family, but "they never became established as the kernel of a set of political preoccupations." Italian filmmaker and poet Pier Paolo Pasolini similarly described the Italian Communist Party as "an island where critical consciousness is always desperately defended: and where human behavior has been still able to preserve the old dignity." In his view, the PCI was

> the saving grace of Italy and its poor democratic institutions . . . a clean country in a dirty country, an honest country in a dishonest country, an intelligent country in an idiotic country, an educated country in an ignorant country, a humanist country in a consumerist country.[27]

By promoting a worldview, political parties helped their members make sense of the world. Opinions were filtered, at times in openly authoritarian ways. Party discipline went hand in hand with intellectual discipline: through ideological training, parties imposed a shared outlook that allowed workers to grasp abstract social processes as amenable to transformation. By contrast, ideological disorientation is a hallmark of the hyperpolitical age. Debate erupts over one issue today, another tomorrow. But individuals no longer possess a heuristic capable of unifying and imposing coherence on their various viewpoints. What emerges instead are fleeting, episodic *partis pris*. In a volume of autobiographical interviews published in the mid-1970s, the German jurist and political scientist Wolfgang Abendroth insisted that rejecting nuclear weapons was all well and good, but one had to reject them from the *correct class standpoint* and situate the question within the broader condition of the working class in West Germany, the United States, and the Soviet Union.[28] Today, almost no one in the opinion-saturated terrain of social media could plausibly derive a coherent stance on COVID restrictions, gas heating, and gender-neutral language from a single, unified position.

For Pasolini and Eribon, the party offered a refuge from a latent loneliness omnipresent in modernity, a haven from the horrors of a "purely private life." These modes of affiliation were not exclusive to the left. Throughout the first half of the twentieth century, the right erected an equally formidable line of fortifications across capitalist society, anchored around churches and neighborhood clubs. The authors of the Marienthal study, quoted above, enumerate a partial list:

> On the Christian Socialist side are the party organization, the Christian Women's Association, the Girls' Club, the Boys' Club, and the child welfare committee called Happy Childhood. On the German Nationalist side are the German *Turn Verein* (Athletic Club) and the German *Gesangs Verein* (Glee Club). The last-named societies are gradually being merged with the recently founded local branch of the National Socialist Party.[29]

From rural women's associations in Bavaria to Vrouw and Maatschappij (Woman and Society), a Christian democratic organization in Flanders, and the Primrose League in Britain, conservative parties practiced a similarly closed form of mass political organization. "Everything was Catholic in the experience of a Catholic," a Dutch journalist recalled of her upbringing, "and one was a Christian twenty-four hours a day."[30]

This landscape began to fissure in the 1980s and 1990s. In France its decline is usually dated to the Mitterrand years, when the far-right National Front first gained a foothold in national politics. Encouraged by Mitterrand himself, who was searching for a cause for his Socialist government after accomplishing its market turn, Le Pen's party would increasingly compete with the left for the support of working-class voters like Eribon's father. The resulting transfer of partisan allegiances entailed a shift in register, as well. "Unlike voting Communist, a way of voting that could be assumed forthrightly and asserted publicly," Eribon wrote, "voting for the extreme right seems to have been something that needed to be kept secret, even denied in the face of some 'outside' instance of judgment."[31] At antipodes to the culture of French Communism, in "voting for the National Front, individuals remain individuals and the opinion they produce is simply the sum of their spontaneous prejudices," an act of defiance carried out in the solitude of the polling booth.

The golden age of party democracy described by Eribon was, of course, no irenic idyll. In France itself, the Fifth Republic issued from a Gaullist coup d'état that introduced a semipresidential system with patently authoritarian features. Dictatorships ruled Greece, Spain, and Portugal for long stretches of the Cold War. At the height of the Trente Glorieuses, European powers fought bitter counterinsurgencies to forestall the independence of their remaining colonial possessions in Africa. Patriarchal structures dominated domestic life, while women were expected to submit to their male breadwinners. Well into the second half of the twentieth century, Flemish and Italian priests told their congregants how to vote, while party bosses dictated editorials to newspaper editors. The Tangentopoli scandal of the early 1990s exposed Italy's *partitocrazia* as flamboyantly corrupt. As a character declares in Belgian writer Hugo Claus's best-known novel, published in 1983: "It's all politics . . . and we're sick of politics!"

A decade later, however, this outburst already found a different resonance. At its postwar peak, the PCI boasted more than

2 million members; by 1990, that number had fallen by almost half—soon after, it was subsumed into the Partito Democratico. In the UK, Labour Party membership declined steadily from over 1 million in 1953 until 1980, when it plunged sharply, falling below 200,000 for the first time in 2006. The Dutch Partij van de Arbeid had 147,000 members in 1959; by the 2000s, only 6,000 remained. Between 1976 and 2005, the German SPD shrank from 1 million members to 572,000, as the average age of party members rose. By 1994, when Achille Occhetto flew to Wall Street, the billionaire telepopulist Silvio Berlusconi was promoting a "people's capitalism" on his privately owned TV channels, flanked by scantily clad female presenters. A capitalist comet had hit the West and killed the dinosaurs; the postpolitical ice age had begun.

The career of parties in the mass-political age can be schematized into several sub-phases. Early on came the creeping "oligarchization" of social democratic parties, described as early as 1911 by the German-Italian sociologist Robert Michels. As suffrage expanded and they were integrated into official politics, party apparatuses increasingly detached themselves from their base. The retention of power became more important than social transformation; "party functionary" evolved into a job description in its own right. Around 1960, parties that had once fought for the particular interests of specific milieus or classes transformed into "catch-all parties" (a term coined by the German political scientist Otto Kirchheimer), aiming to appeal to broader swaths of the electorate. From the 1970s onward, these catch-all parties then mutated into "cartel parties," more interested in access to the levers of state power than ideological competition. Ideological differences faded, and politicians found themselves inclined to collaborate with their supposed adversaries in coalitions of various kinds, motivated by a collusive interest in holding onto ministerial appointments. Parties of the left in particular gradually severed their ties to labor unions and civil society organizations.

The result of this hollowing out of European party politics was aptly described by the Irish political scientist Peter Mair as "ruling the void."[32] Since parties were no longer attuned to the desires and demands of their constituents, other channels had to be tapped, most often PR consultants who relied on focus groups, opinion polls, and open primaries. New Labour under Tony Blair proved particularly adept at the strategy. Consultants, of course, cost money—but the new model was organizationally less demanding than the older system of mass membership. Instead of mobilizing thousands of supporters and party members at meetings and congresses where they could exert pressure on politicians, it was easier to treat the electorate like a black box from which one hopes to extract insight after a plane crash. The Hungarian theorist Péter Csigó speaks of a "neopopular bubble"; in late-modern democracies, politicians were bound to speculate about "the people," party members, and potential voters.[33] In this respect, they came to resemble actors in the ascendant financial sector. That tropes and metaphors from the economy recur here will surprise no one. Political scientists had already begun to frame electoral competition in terms of supply and demand by the 1950s; by the 1980s, politics itself was a market form. Postpolitics triumphed across every layer of society.

In undergraduate political science textbooks, American parties are often regarded as an exception to this European norm. The United States never developed a labor movement of comparable strength and, with few exceptions, never had real mass parties.[34] After the defeat of the populist People's Party—crushed in the South by voter suppression and rifles, in the North by apathy—the cadres of the Democratic and Republican parties constructed a system that made it nearly impossible for others to pose a serious challenge. Yet even the duopolists were once rooted in a wider array of grassroots organizations. During the New Deal era, the Democratic Party could, through its alliances with unions and other associations, plausibly be seen as a rough equivalent to European parties. The Detroit union leader Walter Reuther marched in the 1960s alongside Martin Luther King; one of the main backers of King's 1963 March on Washington was A. Philip Randolph, a radical trade unionist who had been organizing black workers since the 1920s. Although the Democratic Party's relationship to these forces was always serpentine and stepmotherly, they helped ensure that it remained a "party of workers" without ever becoming a "workers' party."

By the 1970s, this landscape had started to desiccate. The democratic promise Alexis de Tocqueville once saw in the United States—and that generations of European travelers had reported on—was supplanted by the reality described by Putnam, in which people bowled, worked, and voted alone. Whereas millions of Americans were still active in membership-based organizations in the 1960s, an epochal restructuring of group life now went into effect. On the one hand, the menu of political issues visibly broadened. Theda Skocpol points to the proliferation of "environmental groups, antipoverty groups, pro-choice and pro-life groups, family values groups, and associations dealing with the rights of women, racial and ethnic minorities, and other vulnerable categories of Americans."[35]

In Skocpol's assessment, however, another change proved to be just as significant: citizens who did seek to be politically involved no longer followed the classical model. "Although thousands of new, nationally visible groups were created between the 1960s and the 1990s," she writes, "many—such as public law groups, think tanks, foundations, and political action committees—are not membership groups at all."[36] They no longer had structures with local branches, and their political work was carried out by professional staff. The change occurred with such rapidity, Skocpol notes, that it cannot be explained merely by generational turnover or individual choices. Rather, a highly educated elite of Americans, disillusioned by the Vietnam War, withdrew from cross-class membership associations and instead built professionally managed organizations. The nonprofit model also offered the advantage of tax benefits. These organizations were not financed through dues but turned to wealthy donors. Skocpol refers to such NGOs as "advocates without members"—lawyers speaking on behalf of defendants who, for the most part, would remain mute and passive.[37] Together with PR consultants and technocrats, they made up the ghost armies of postpolitics.

As parties and political associations rewrote their contract with citizens, so too did they refigure their relationship to the state. In the era of postpolitics, a chasm opened between two dimensions of the political: politics and policy (the notion of polity, invoked by Sloterdijk, here completes the triad). Policy encompasses the methods by which states organize their societies, such as choosing winners and losers in industrial policy. Politics pertains to campaigning, competition between parties, forging alliances and coalitions. In the 1990s, these two dimensions came to interact in a radically different mode. Policy became the purview of unelected actors—central banks and bodies such as the European Commission—morphing into what would soon be termed technocracy. Politics was relegated to a media sphere addicted to novelty, supplemented somewhat hopefully by the participatory promise of Web 2.0.

Here the economic drivers of Putnam's crisis slide into full view. Unsurprisingly, the classical mass party was often analogized to a factory hall. Both had a strict, almost military set-up in which militants and leaders had a well-defined hierarchy and division of labor. These parties also defended clearly delineated interest groups in society: employees and employers, middle and lower strata, Protestants and Catholics. When they came to power, they satisfied their respective clienteles with the expected prebendary services, an arrangement that worked as long as government revenues increased in step with economic growth. With the end of the boom in the early 1970s, this capacity diminished. Conservatives, who blamed loose monetary policy for rampant inflation, declared democracy to be in crisis. The infamous 1975 report of the Trilateral Commission, a think tank dedicated to promoting co-ordination between elites in the US, Japan, and Europe, provided the canonical statement of this alarmism. Its conclusion, jointly authored by Samuel P. Huntington, Michel Crozier, and Joji Watanuki, read:

> Inflation is obviously not a problem which is peculiar to democratic societies, and it may well be the result of causes quite extrinsic to the democratic process. It may, however, be exacerbated by a democratic politics and it is, without doubt, extremely difficult for democratic systems to deal with effectively. The natural tendency of the political demands permitted and encouraged by the dynamics of a democratic system helps governments to deal with the problems of economic recession, particularly unemployment, and it hampers them in dealing effectively with inflation. In the face of the claims of business groups, labor unions, and the beneficiaries of governmental largesse, it becomes difficult if not impossible for democratic governments to curtail spending, increase taxes, and control prices and wages. In this sense, inflation is the economic disease of democracies.[38]

Behind this diagnosis already lay the premises of a conscious class strategy. If the demands of overly entitled citizens represented by strong mass parties had provoked an inflationary spiral and driven states to the precipice of ungovernability, the power of trade unions furnished another target for the neoliberal offensive that gained momentum from the mid-1970s. Faced with sluggish growth and pressure on capital accumulation, businesses unilaterally cancelled the postwar compact. To increase profits, or at least to arrest further decline, required a reduction in the wage share, supposedly artificially maintained by labor "cartels." If breaking the unions dealt a blow to other institutions, so be it.

Moreover, the timing seemed uniquely favorable for such an offensive. The long downturn left many organizations with less room to maneuver, in particular on the left. A booming economy could tolerate higher wages and thus higher membership dues. Now these funds started to dry up. The political scientist Thomas Ferguson notes that "the deterioration of the network of community groups generated in the course of the struggles over the rights of blacks, women, and poor" resulted in part from the receding economic tide. These groups had "flourished in the turbulent 1960s, when the economy was expanding and substantial financial assistance was available from the government and large foundations."[39] In the following decades, little resistance was to be expected from that quarter.

To maintain monetary stability, the left's mass-political organizations thus had to be rendered invertebrate. Under its new chairman Paul Volcker, the US Federal Reserve raised the base interest rate from 11 to 20 percent between 1979 and 1981, drastically reordering the economic landscape. Flood gave way to drought. The Volcker Shock triggered a recession, unemployment soared, and accelerated deindustrialization—"politics put in the service of its own negation," in the words of French philosopher Marcel Gauchet.[40]

Fortuitously, from the perspective of the conservative camp, the mass organizations which had brought state and capital to this impasse were already faltering due to the processes of social recomposition registered by Putnam. Politically orchestrated crackdowns further depleted their resources. In 1981, Reagan ended the air traffic controllers' strike; four years later, Thatcher cracked the spine of the mighty British Miners' Association. English writer James Heartfield described the upshot:

> To defeat the working-class challenge of the seventies, the elite tore up the old institutions that bound the masses to the state. Class conflict was institutionalized under the old system, which not only contained working-class opposition but also helped the ruling class to formulate a common outlook.

In doing so, however, conservatives overshot the mark:

> What started as an offensive against working class solidarity in the eighties undermined the institutions that bound society together. Not just trade unions and socialist parties were undermined, but so too were right-wing political parties and their traditional support bases amongst church and farmers' groups.[41]

At the turn of the millennium, Putnam already coupled his social-scientific analysis with a bleak prognosis for American democracy in the new century. The subsequent rise of populism in Europe and the Trump phenomenon in the US invited interpretation along similar lines, as consequences of the decline of communal life following the controlled demolition of the public sphere in the 1980s and 1990s. Only through the erosion of social capital, it was said, had this new form of ressentiment-driven politics become possible. Some observers even discerned the danger of a return of fascism: according to the historian Timothy Snyder and the philosopher Jason Stanley, figures like Trump and Jair Bolsonaro stand in direct continuity with the demagogic personages of the 1930s.[42] The Trump presidency, Snyder wrote after the storming of the Capitol on January 6, 2021, represented "the original sin of American history in the post-slavery era, our closest brush with fascism so far."[43] Snyder still spoke of "pre-fascism," however, because "for a coup to work in 2024, the breakers will require something that Trump never quite had: an angry minority, organized for nationwide violence, ready to add intimidation to an election . . . Four years of amplifying a big lie just might get them this." Journalists Paul Mason and Sarah Kendzior published manuals on how this new fascism could be stopped in its tracks; former US Secretary of State Madeleine Albright presented herself as antifascist-in-chief.[44]

In 2000 already, Putnam himself warned that social capital exhibited a "dark side." "It was social capital, for example, that enabled Timothy McVeigh to bomb the Alfred P. Murrah Federal Building in Oklahoma City," he wrote.[45] "McVeigh's network of friends, bound together by a norm of reciprocity, enabled him to do what he could not have done alone." Other scholars have followed suit. In their much-cited article "Bowling for Fascism," Shanker Satyanath, Nico Voigtländer, and Hans-Joachim Voth marshal regression analyses to show that in the early phase—particularly in *Länder* (federal states) with unstable coalition governments—a higher density of social capital increased the likelihood that people would join the National Socialist German Workers' Party (NSDAP).[46] They explain the correlation in part by noting that the Nazis specifically targeted the leaders of clubs and associations, making connections to help spread the party's message—a tactic employed with success not only in conservative circles but also in apolitical groups like chess or hiking clubs.

A few years later, Andrés Rodriguez-Pose, Neil Lee, and Cornelius Lipp's "Golfing with Trump" adopted a similar approach. They found that in 2016 Trump outperformed the previous Republican presidential candidate, Mitt Romney, in counties with comparatively high concentrations of social capital, particularly in rural areas that had experienced economic and demographic decline. Stagnation, outmigration, and increasing regional inequality, the authors argue, were especially likely to spur populist protest in places where associational life (such as golf clubs) and community life remained relatively intact. In the Rust Belt and the Midwest, communities instead tended to experience individual losses as collective ones. People in small towns—the proverbial flyover country—"have had enough of seeing their people leave and their jobs go and have used the ballot box to exact revenge on a system they consider offers little to them."[47] Such findings present a challenge to a thesis arguing that the hyperpolitical era is characterized by repoliticization in an institutional void. Instead, they suggest that we may be witnessing a process of asymmetric reinstitutionalization and civic renaissance, at least on the right—seen from this angle, hyperpolitics itself may soon be history.

Is Trump a fascist? And is Trumpism the result of a deserted social landscape and postpolitical atomization, or is its success rooted in a relatively intact right-wing civil society? The philosopher Alberto Toscano answered the first question in the affirmative, positing a form of "racial fascism."[48] Historian Gabriel Winant concurs, and he goes on to outline the associative foundations of Trump's coalition. "The primary factor of social cohesion in Tocqueville's America was nothing other than white supremacy," Winant contends, and "given that this structure has endured, it makes little sense to imagine our society as formerly rich with association but now bereft of it."[49] With reference to the couple who, in the summer of 2020, emerged from their home armed with an assault rifle and a pistol to threaten participants in a passing Black Lives Matter demonstration, Winant notes that the

> gun-waving McCloskeys in St. Louis are presumably not members of the same kind of fraternal organizations that were popular in the 19th century, but they are members of a home-owners' association. Whiteness itself is a kind of inchoate associational gel, out of which a variety of more specific associations may grow in a given historical conjuncture.[50]

The logic appears irresistible: if Trump looks like a racial fascist, swims like a racial fascist, and quacks like a racial fascist, then he probably is a racial fascist. Voices in high quarters have seconded Winant on this point: in a September 2022 speech, for instance, President Biden castigated MAGA Republicans as a "threat to our very democracy," evidence of a drift toward "semi-fascism."[51]

On the other side of this debate stand critics like political scientist Corey Robin and sociologist Dylan Riley, for whom the Trump phenomenon is better theorized as a species of late-modern authoritarianism that shares little with the "superpoliticized" fascisms of the interbellum period.[52] Riley charges the proponents of the Trump-as-fascist diagnosis with a failure to locate their analogies "in a properly comparative and historical perspective."[53] "Instead," he writes, "they treat the past as a storehouse of disconnected examples." Classical fascism, Riley argues, as it took root in interwar Italy and Germany, can only be understood in connection with the First World War and the menace of socialist revolution, where unemployed veterans formed the core of fascist gangs that attacked leftist activists. Moreover, fascists learned from their adversaries and built disciplined mass parties of their own. By these standards, present-day right-wing populism clearly lacks some essential criteria: there is no prerevolutionary working class poised for power, and no polity in the West has experienced total war, with its brutalizing initiation into the exercise of violence. Finally, as Heinrich Geiselberger has observed, today's right largely lacks disciplined mass organizations. In their place, the far right resembles "a swarm rather than a choreographed formation, with porous borders between gravity and earnestness, sincerity and irony."[54]

Riley finds a more apt analogy in Bonapartism, iconically described by Marx in *The Eighteenth Brumaire of Louis Bonaparte*. Where Trump casts himself as champion of the victims of globalization, Louis Napoleon relied on the largely passive support of impoverished peasants, not a collective but "formed by the simple addition of isomorphous magnitudes, much as potatoes in a sack form a sack of potatoes."

> They cannot represent themselves; they must be represented. Their representative must appear simultaneously as their master, as an authority over them, an unrestricted governmental power that protects them from the other classes and sends them rain and sunshine from above. The political influence of the small peasant proprietors is therefore ultimately expressed in the executive subordinating society to itself.[55]

The family resemblances are not hard to register. In his first term, Trump resorted to so-called executive orders more frequently than his immediate predecessors, bypassing Congress and asserting presidential authority to enact laws by decree—what some observers saw as an expression of "plutocratic authoritarianism."[56] Trump's power, and that of the Republican right, does not rest on large majorities in the population or a strong mass movement. George W. Bush did not win a majority of the popular vote in the 2000 election; in 2024, Trump overtook his rival by a hair's breadth, with 49.8 percent. American conservatism, Robin argues, is "no longer a movement in ascendancy," and even between 2016 and 2018—when Republicans controlled their trifecta in the White House, Senate, and House of Representatives—they struggled to implement substantial parts of their agenda.[57] As a political project, it relies on antiquated provisions of the US Constitution originally designed to shield elite interests from the majority of the population, such as the disproportionate influence of sparsely populated states in the Senate and the Electoral College, or lifetime appointments to the Supreme Court. Robin calls this "gonzo constitutionalism." Although MAGA Republicans are portrayed by their opponents as "lawless enemies of the Constitution" bolstered by a "combination of rabid rhetoric and mobilized masses," their actual power depends "upon the constitutional mainstays we learned about in high-school civics."[58] "Semi-fascism" may be a rhetorically convenient term for this phenomenon, but in the end, there is no night in which all cows are black.

Ultimately, the debate over whether Trump, Bolsonaro, and co. should be considered modern reincarnations of fascism may seem scholastic. More significant, however, is the question of whether phenomena like Trumpism reflect a replenishment of social capital and a reinstitutionalization of political participation—whether, in other words, Putnam's thesis is at least partially being falsified. While Riley and Robin reject said interpretation, insisting on the weakness of the Republican Party, Winant's argument and studies like "Golfing with Trump" point in the opposite direction. Communal ties and dense associational networks, they suggest, are an important resource for right-wing Republicans; radicalized conservatism is a dynamic social movement, reinforced by institutions such as homeowners' associations and the "binding glue" of whiteness.

Empirical studies measure social capital with specific indices. Rodríguez-Pose, Lee, and Lipp, for instance, use four variables: the number of nonprofit organizations in a county, the 2010 census response rate, voter turnout in the 2016 presidential election, and the prevalence of associational indicators that include not only gyms, bowling alleys, and golf clubs but also unions. Ultimately, their findings depend on which phenomena are included in such indices and how different political forms are evaluated. Even if social capital helps to explain the vote for Trump, there is no reason necessarily to expect that it will give rise to durable mass organizations capable of involving people in politics in a way that allows them to influence policy. Amnesty International, after all, is not the Communist Party any more than a golf club is the NSDAP. NGOs run by professional staff are not fortresses of civil society but heads without bodies, recruiting donors rather than members and lacking both the ambition and prospect of uniting a cohesive base.

What about the right's other supposed reserve assets, from homeownership to whiteness? It is undoubtedly true that many right-wing institutions have fared comparatively better in the neoliberal age, when viewed from the desert landscape of the left. But arguments like Winant's make it unclear how we should distinguish between being white and being a member of the Ku Klux Klan. In an age in which legal segregation has been abolished, racial status is no longer the criterion of civic inclusion that it was under Jim Crow.

The KKK and other white-supremacist groups might well count among the first properly fascist organizations in history. But as institutions, they have been on the wane for at least a century, and their days as the stormtroopers of racial hierarchy are long past. Militias like the Proud Boys and the Boogaloo movement, or Germany's *Querfronten*, function as "individualized commandos," as historian Adam Tooze put it, far removed from the veterans that populated the Freikorps or the Black and Tans in the early 1920s.[59] These were disciplined formations with direct experience of combat, not lumpen hobbyists radicalized in a digital echo chamber.

Much the same holds true for Europe's new far right. Giorgia Meloni's postfascist Fratelli d'Italia has grown remarkably in recent years and now leads a governing coalition. Still, it will not soon equal the 230,000 members that its predecessor Italian Social Movement (MSI) had in the early 1960s. If the latest advance for a far-right party in the homeland of fascism "surely lends itself to evocative analogies," historian David Broder writes, "this does not mean that Mussolini's heirs repeat the past in the present" or that their authentically fascist aspects are modeled on Italian precedent.[60]

One can therefore conclude, ambivalently, that even if Trump and other nationalists are indeed supported by a robust associative network, this does not necessarily alter the broader context of demobilization in which they have operated, at least so far. That may in fact be an advantage from their perspective. The right has historically been content to defend existing property relations. Apathy and resignation are its greatest assets, not militancy. It thus remains unclear whether social capital is actually growing on the right or whether it is simply eroding more slowly.

~

One finding remains noteworthy, however, and will be revisited from another angle in the next chapter. In the passage on the right-wing overshoot of the 1980s, James Heartfield records that "the right-wing parties and their traditional base in the church and farmers' organizations" were also hit hard by the capitalist counteroffensive of the 1970s and 1980s. Indeed, in the UK, the Conservatives suffered a dramatic loss in membership, from a staggering 2.8 million in 1953 to just over 170,000 in 2022. As Tariq Ali has written, this self-immolation was a product of Thatcher's market reforms, which led to "the decimation of the Tories' provincial base of local gentry, bank managers and businessmen through the waves of trans-Atlantic acquisitions and privatizations she unleashed." The Iron Lady may have "succeeded in rebooting returns on capital and crushed the organized working class," but at the cost of lasting damage to her party.[61] Both numerically and qualitatively, the English right remains a shadow of its former self. The Primrose League was disbanded in 2004, and anyone visiting rural Britain will quickly notice the faded Conservative Club placards. Those groups which have survived look more like retirement homes than centers of mobilization (the median age of the Conservative Party membership is estimated to be seventy-two). At the same time, however, evidence can be marshaled that the erosion of social capital and deinstitutionalization of political participation are less advanced than on the left. R. W. Johnson observed in 2015 that "the atomization and dispersal of the Labour vote" had led to "whole chunks falling off the side to the SNP and UKIP," while "the institutional base of the Tory Party—private schools, the Anglican Church, wealthy housing districts, the expanded private sector and even home ownership in general—is as healthy as ever." The result was "a one-sided decay of the class cleavage, with the Tories holding onto their old hinterland far better than Labour has."[62] From Oxford's Bullingdon Club to the City guilds, the Conservatives have made an effort to preserve their elite incubators and pools of personnel. Theda Skocpol documents how the US right not only founded new NGOs, foundations, and think tanks but also invested significantly more energy than its rivals in reviving or reinventing "massive and well-established" membership organizations such as the National Rifle Association, which often crossed class boundaries and whose dense networks reached into the "penumbra of the Republican Party." The sociologist César Rendueles makes a similar point when he claimed that the "upper classes managed to shield themselves from postmodern individualization by preserving their social capital—for example, through elite educational establishments or affinity networks bound up with lifestyle—a simulacrum of a cultural project, based on sophisticated consumption."[63]

Why, then, has the right fared better than the left in Putnam's postpolitical ice age? The answer may be more straightforward than it appears. Conservatism has always grown organically out of capitalist society, soldered by the default forms of association that capital generates. As Engels pointed out in an 1881 report to British trade unionists, the ruling class here enjoys a structural advantage:

> Capitalists are always organized. They need in most cases no formal union, no rules, officers, etc. Their small number, as compared with that of the workman, the fact of their forming a separate class, their constant social and commercial intercourse stand them in lieu of that . . . On the other hand, the workpeople from the very beginning cannot do without a strong organization, well-defined by rules and delegating its authority to officers and committees . . . The formerly helpless mass, divided against itself, was no longer so.[64]

As Engels already intimated, the crisis of civil society diagnosed by Putnam would pose a greater problem for the left, since the bar for success is inevitably set higher.

All the same, deinstitutionalization has not left the right entirely untouched. This is evident in the rapid turnover at the top of the Tory Party, as well as in GOP leaders' frustration at the lack of discipline on the part of fervent Trump supporters in the legislature. In January 2023, Republican Congressman Kevin McCarthy needed no fewer than fifteen rounds of voting to be elected Speaker of the House; in an unprecedented motion, members of his own party voted to oust him from the position before the year was up. As Paul Heideman has written, the taming of labor removed the external constraints that once disciplined capitalists and motivated them to maintain unity and pursue a common agenda.[65] Without a worthy adversary to concentrate the mind, internal fractures are likely to widen—between "woke" capital and the Koch brothers, DeSantis and Disneyland, Elon Musk and Steve Bannon—and the contemporary state can no longer fulfill its role as guarantor or *Gesamtkapitalist.* Given the "weakening of the parties since the 1970s, and the political disorganization of corporate America since the 1980s," as the academic Cathie Jo Martin has argued, "it is much harder for US employers to think about their collective long-term interests."[66] Rather than a realignment—that is, a strategic shift of the working class toward the Republican Party, as some observers have suggested—we are instead witnessing dealignment, the relentless and accelerating dissolution of existing party affiliations.[67]

3

The Antipolitical Decade

The year 2010 was a good one for Michel Houellebecq. His novel *The Map and the Territory*, published in September, topped the bestseller lists for months. "In 2010, I won the Prix Goncourt; France didn't do too well in the World Cup; and Apple launched its iPad," he later remarked about an otherwise uneventful calendar.[1]

Houellebecq's run of good luck was abruptly interrupted when the spotlight shifted to an unlikely competitor. In October, ninety-three-year-old Resistance veteran and former UN diplomat Stéphane Hessel published a short pamphlet titled *Indignez-vous!* (*Time for Outrage!*), which sold a million copies within weeks. Hessel struck a deeply un-Houellebecquian tone: he called on Western citizens to rise up against their political elites and to halt the West's slide into economic apartheid. "The worst attitude," he wrote, "is indifference." "'There's nothing I can do; I get by'—adopting this mindset will deprive you of one of the fundamental qualities of being human: outrage."[2] Observers were perplexed: "At the very moment the dark oracle Michel Houellebecq storms the literary charts with his neurasthenic, museumified France," wrote one journalist, "a remarkable little book of just thirty pages has held the top spot on the nonfiction bestseller list for weeks."[3]

~

Hessel's book landed in a political climate undergoing spasmodic change. Ever since reporter Rick Santelli called for a "Chicago Tea Party" live from the trading floor in February 2009 against Obama administration's bailout plans, the Tea Party movement had been driving Republican lawmakers ahead of it, pressuring them to block Obama's legislation and nearly pushing the United States into default in the summer of 2011. In October 2009, Italian comedian Beppe Grillo—who had already staged a first Vaffanculo (Fuck-off) Day in 2007 in protest of political corruption—founded the ideologically amorphous Five Star Movement (M5S) together with internet entrepreneur Gianroberto Casaleggio. From December 2010, mass protests erupted in North Africa and the Middle East, beginning in Tunisia; in Cairo, demonstrators occupied Tahrir Square, and long-standing Egyptian president Hosni Mubarak stepped down in February. In May 2011, demonstrations by the Indignados—the "outraged"—took place in cities across Spain, citing Hessel as an inspiration; at the same time, angry citizens in Athens protested on Syntagma Square against their government's austerity policies. In mid-September, Occupy Wall Street protesters occupied Zuccotti Park in Lower Manhattan. Four weeks later, activists set up camp outside Saint Paul's Cathedral in London. "People are waking up from their coma," read one placard. At the end of December, *Time* magazine named "The Protester" as its Person of the Year. After the Russian presidential elections in spring 2012, mass demonstrations broke out in Moscow, and in May 2013, anti-Erdoğan activists invaded Gezi Park in Istanbul.

The new sensibility eventually seeped into Houellebecq's work, after some delay. As late as 2015, the protagonist of *Submission* looked back on a world where elections "could not have been less interesting; the mediocrity of the 'political offerings' was almost surprising."

> A center-left candidate would be elected, serve either one or two terms, depending how charismatic he was, then for obscure reasons he would fail to complete a third. When people got tired of that candidate, and the center-left in general, we'd witness the phenomenon of *democratic change*, and the voters would install a candidate of the center-right, also for one or two terms, depending on his personal appeal. Western nations took a strange pride in this system, though it amounted to little more than a power-sharing deal between two rival gangs, and they would even go to war to impose it on nations that failed to share their enthusiasm.[4]

Four years later, in *Serotonin*, Houellebecq's characters are loudly contemplating their nation's exit from the European Union, and armed farmers assault police on the autoroute. The novelist's seismograph had picked up the last tremors of the postpolitical moment.

Between postpolitics and hyperpolitics lies the antipolitical decade, an intermediate phase heralded by the success of Hessel's pamphlet and the protests that rippled across the globe from 2010 onwards. The progressive-neoliberal consensus of the long 1990s released its hegemonic grip; left- and right-wing movements destabilized the established party systems, a process that eventually culminated in the populist victories of 2016 and beyond.

Taking the incidence of demonstrations and spontaneous strikes as an indicator of repoliticization, the results are unequivocal, even spectacular (see Figure 2). After a prolonged period of low and declining protest activity—interrupted only briefly around the year 2000, when alter-globalists demonstrated against summits in Seattle and Genoa—protest levels surged dramatically from 2010 onward.

Figure 2: Strikes, Demonstrations, and Armed Conflict Worldwide, 1995–2015

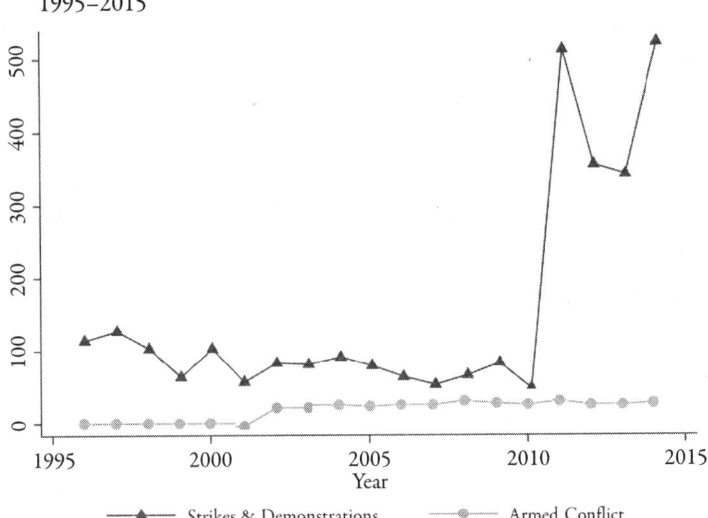

The political-economic background to this upsurge is plain to see. Although economic growth in OECD countries had already entered its phase of secular stagnation in the 1970s, although center-right parties and centrist Social Democrats had already rolled back much of the mass-political welfare state, and although inequality had been rising for some time, neoliberalism's ideological hegemony remained unbroken for a long while. Atomized citizens continued to subscribe to meritocratic norms, attributing personal failure more to themselves than to politics or capitalism. On the other side of the ledger, governments managed to cushion social hardship through rising public debt and, later, easier access to private credit—what the British political scientist Colin Crouch described as "privatized Keynesianism." In 2008, this entire debt-based regime blew apart with the subprime mortgage crisis: banks collapsed and debtors were forced to auction off their homes when they could no longer service their loans, whereafter states intervened to bail out the banks and establish financial rescue packages. When international capital markets froze, net importers—such as many dictatorships in North Africa and the Middle East—could no longer control prices for food and other basic goods to pacify their populations. Bread riots followed, and soon afterward, relatively well-educated but directionless youth took to the streets, demanding change at the top. They appeared as the vanguard of a Facebook *fronde*, enlisting in a "revolution without revolutionaries."

What effects would this repoliticization have, and what institutional forms would it take? Left parties of the mass-political era were born out of spontaneous, decentralized movements before becoming formalized, oligarchized, and eventually cartelized. Were we now witnessing the birth phase of new mass organizations—a new cycle in the making? If, to borrow Sloterdijk's formulation, parties serve as "deposit banks for public rage" that collect affects and convert them into political capital, how would the established parties relate to the movements, and vice versa? And, most importantly, how would these movements grapple with the Putnamite slump in civic activity?

As a term, "antipolitics" is intrinsically ambiguous, and its history includes an intriguing twist or semantic shift. It was coined in the 1980s by dissident intellectuals in the Soviet bloc. As Hungarian writer György Konrád wrote in a now-classic essay:

> In Eastern Europe, we are not primarily concerned with the question of whether politics is good or bad, but with the fact that we are surrounded everywhere by too much, all too much politics. The state draws countless matters, questions and decisions into the realm of politics that have no place there. Private

> matters and specialist questions that ultimately have nothing to do with the state.[5]

Konrad's immediate target was the state-socialist regimes that had colonized social life with their parties and mass organizations—what they bequeathed was, quite literally, the surfeit lamented in Hugo Claus's 1983 novel. In its stead, Konrád called for a depoliticized zone, a space where writers and intellectuals could express themselves without fear of censure:

> Anti-politics is the politicization of people who do not want to become politicians or take a share of power. Anti-politics pursues the creation of independent agencies vis-à-vis political power, anti-politics is a counter-power that cannot come to power and does not want to. Anti-politics already possesses power because of its sheer moral and cultural weight.

After the fall of the Wall and the Velvet Revolution in his own country, Václav Havel—the writer and later president of Czechoslovakia in December 1989—reflected in a speech in Prague that during the years of dissent and opposition, "the struggle we waged had nothing in common with the word 'politics.'" "We used the term 'non-political politics' and 'antipolitics.'" This was about "principles and values, not about power and positions." The challenge now, he continued, was not to betray its legacy even in high office—or at least to engage with it productively: "From my early experiences, I can say that the fact that we now find ourselves in an entirely different environment . . . cannot change the essence of our efforts and ideals; it can only change the form in which they are realized."[6] The prefix "*anti-*," for this tradition, thus denoted resistance to classical mass politics in its actually existing socialist form. As dissidents, Konrád and

Havel then sought precisely the type of freedom that would define the nascent age of postpolitics—a form of politics directed against the institutions of mass politics, intended to foster moral experimentation.

When observers began applying the term "antipolitics" to the protest movements that coalesced after 2008, they did so independently of this earlier Eastern European iteration. Their antipolitics instead referred to a different type of antagonism, unmissable in the slogans of the Indignados or Occupy Wall Street. The Occupy protesters identified as part of the "99 percent," challenging the domination of the "1 percent." Spanish demonstrators chanted "¡Que se vayan todos!" (They should all go!) and "¡No nos representan!" (They don't represent us!), with framing which opposed *el pueblo* (the people) to *la casta* (the caste) of capitalists, technocrats, and politicians. The "*anti-*" here was directed against the status quo, against elites, against the establishment, an orientation also visible in the definition of populism proffered by political scientists such as Cas Mudde, Cristóbal Rovira Kaltwasser, and Jan-Werner Müller, who declared it a "thin ideology" based, in Müller's words, on "an opposition between corrupt elites and a morally pure, homogeneous people that can do no wrong."[7]

Populism had already, in the early years of crisis, become something of a hate-object for elites. When a journalist from the *Frankfurter Allgemeine Zeitung* asked Belgian EU Council President Herman Van Rompuy in 2010 what he considered the greatest threat to Europe, Van Rompuy replied laconically, with the success of the Vlaams Belang party in mind: "The great danger is populism."[8] The term "populism" underwent a remarkable boom: whereas around 200 English-language publications had mentioned the p-word in 1960, by the mid-2010s the figure had climbed to nearly 800.[9] In 2017, the Cambridge Dictionary named it word of the year; in November 2018, the *Guardian* devoted a special dossier to the phenomenon in the form of a quiz.[10] Political-scientific terms both reflect and shape the world that produces them, and the uptake of the word "populism" marked a much deeper structural trend: across the globe, political entrepreneurs and parties claiming to speak in the name of the people won majorities, unseated incumbents, and attacked the independence of the judiciary.

Was it possible, some were led to ask, to add anything meaningful to the mountain of literature on the *p*-word? Bookstore shelves overflowing with works on populist "explosions," "threats," and "dangers" suggested that the populism industry, especially in academia—its principal stronghold—had reached a point of saturation by the time of the Trump/Brexit moment. "Populism," Gáspár Miklós Tamás wrote sarcastically in 2017, "now stands for 'I don't know what it is, but I was asked to talk about it.'"[11] By the middle of the decade, populists had come to constitute one of the political species coinhabiting the ecosystem of disorganized democracy, alongside NGO functionaries, corporate managers, and liberal technocrats.

One of the first to classify the new movements of the 2010s as a form of antipolitics was the French legal historian Jacques de Saint Victor. In 2014, he saw in Beppe Grillo's rise as the sign that a "new chapter seems to be turning in the history of our democracies." "Twenty years of 'politics as spectacle,' mockery and technocratic excesses," Saint Victor argued, "have produced an aggrieved populace who, whether hyperactive or apathetic, out of protest or sheer disgust, are turning above all against their elites . . . whom they accuse of having betrayed and abandoned them."

> The word [antipolitics] is ambiguous but apt. It expresses a type of moral indignation and rebellion on the part of a growing number of fringe groups who seek to free themselves from the old politics, chiefly through the supposed "virtues" of the Internet. For a long time, prior to the advent of the interactive web, or Web 2.0 (YouTube, Facebook, Twitter, etc.), this diffuse mood of protest only manifested itself in abstention from voting, sometimes understood as "negative politicization," or in the drift toward "populism" of the Lega Nord variety.[12]

In the 1980s, Konrád and Havel had protested an excess of politics. Now the angry citizens of the West were protesting its cruel absence, barely concealed by PR campaigns justifying austerity policies. Alex Hochuli, George Hoare, and Philip Cunliffe describe the mechanism succinctly: "The strategy of depoliticization known as post-politics breeds an angry reaction: the institutions of formal politics come to be rejected by citizens. At the End of the End of History, antipolitics becomes the predominant force."[13]

Saint Victor likewise contended that antipolitics emanated from "fringe groups," but did the postpolitical ice cap really start to thaw from the edges? Public discourse often vaguely and condescendingly identifies "losers" of globalization or modernization as the social base of populist mobilization. Many commentators no doubt have in mind laid-off or embattled industrial workers like Didier Eribon's father. But if we look at the Tea Party and Occupy Wall Street as paradigmatic examples of right- and left-wing antipolitics respectively, it remains striking that historically proletarian strata did not occupy the front ranks of protest, or at least not visibly. What stands out are the different middle-class factions. The German sociologist Nils C. Kumkar, who devoted a comparative study to these movements, concluded that two "intermediate classes," or groups in "contradictory class positions," were decisive:[14] on the one hand, the traditional conservative petty bourgeoisie; on the other, a historically younger petite bourgeoisie. Behind the Tea Party, Kumkar argues, stood craftsmen and small-business owners whose "economic base was gradually eroded by the process of capitalist accumulation."[15] The new petty bourgeoisie, by contrast, consisted of salaried employees who "capitalize their knowledge, have a relatively high degree of autonomy in their work and sometimes the power to organize the production process themselves." In the wake of the Great Financial Crisis, these younger cohorts faced high student debt and bleak job prospects. The core of Occupy was thus made up of the "proletarianized" and "biographically blocked aspiring new petite bourgeoisie," protesting the "devaluation of the cultural capital they had accumulated"[16]—a finding that can probably be applied, *cum grano salis*, to the demonstrators in Spain and Greece as well: academically credentialed millennials who, after the Euro crisis and its accompanying austerity programs, saw little hope of securing adequate employment and soon left their countries in droves. These twin factions of the middle class now vented their displeasure at progressive neoliberalism, with an older middle class tending to resist the progressive component and the new middle class the neoliberal part.

The contrast recalls the question of how repoliticized antipolitical movements fared under conditions of diminished social capital, deinstitutionalized political participation, and new digital media, and how they dealt with the transformed social landscape. Inevitably, we must here distinguish between the early, organic phase of grassroots mobilization and a second stage in which other actors also attempted to ride the antipolitical wave.

~

After protesters occupied Zuccotti Park in September 2011, images of helter-skelter ebullience spread across the globe. People recounted personal experiences as members of "the 99 percent"; since electronic amplification was not permitted, their statements were relayed via a "people's mic" across the square. "I just showed up," recalled the anarchist anthropologist David Graeber of those first meetings, and protesters there spontaneously "decided to have a real assembly."[17] When labor unions and Democratic Party figures such as then–House Speaker Nancy Pelosi expressed solidarity with the encampment, they found themselves brusquely rejected. Beyond the demand for debt relief, the demonstrators did not put forward any concrete agenda, refused any institutional leadership or "vertical interference," and strictly adhered to horizontalist principles. For Graeber, Occupy was defiantly "prefigurative."[18] "If you make demands," he said, "you're asking the people in power and the existing institutions to do something different. And one reason people have been hesitant to do that is they see these institutions as the problem." The Slovenian philosopher Slavoj Žižek was reminded of a "happening in the hippy style of the 1960s: 'They are asking us what our program is. We have no program. We are here to have a good time.'"[19] Žižek warned early on of the fecklessness of this attitude. In a speech given on site in New York in October 2011, he cautioned the assembled Occupiers that

> carnivals come cheap. What matters is the day after, when we will have to return to normal lives . . . there is a long road ahead. There are many truly difficult questions that confront us. We know what we do not want. But what do we want? What social organization can replace capitalism? What type of new leaders do we want?[20]

Interest in questions of political economy and social inequality did blossom in the aftermath of the occupations; tomes such as David Graeber's *Debt* (2011) and Thomas Piketty's *Capital in the Twenty-First Century* (2013) became global bestsellers, shifting the terms of Western debate. Institutionally, however, little came of it. The park was cleared in mid-November and the movement, deliberately resistant to formalization, gradually dissolved—at least for the time being.

In Greece, developments followed a sensitively different course. There, a small party already in existence—Syriza, an electoral alliance formed in 2004 from a dozen communist and post-Trotskyist groupings—succeeded in channeling the new antipolitical energies. With both center-left PASOK and its right-wing rival New Democracy having either failed to manage the fallout from the financial crisis or capitulated to the austerity demands of the so-called troika (made up of the European Commission, the European Central Bank, and the IMF), Syriza leader Alexis Tsipras led the party to second place in the 2012 elections and to a resounding victory in January 2015, becoming prime minister. Together with his finance minister Yanis Varoufakis, Tsipras opposed the dictates of the European Commission and the IMF, briefly making him a global symbol of anti-neoliberal defiance. For a moment, it appeared that antipolitical affect could be successfully converted into power through the classical transmission belt of the party. In July 2015, the Greek electorate rejected the reforms proposed by the Euro establishment. Tsipras had reached the apex of his popularity, only to reverse course out of fear of a Grexit. Syriza itself soon transformed into a conventional cartel party; the leadership distanced itself from the rank and file, and its support cratered. In the 2019 elections it again fell behind New Democracy. By June 2023, ND leader Kyriakos

Mitsotakis had consolidated his majority, while to the party's right, the ultranationalist Spartans entered parliament. Syriza, by contrast, fell to just under 18 percent. The party retained some popularity among younger voters, but lost ground in the working-class districts of the major cities, many of whose residents returned to PASOK.[21]

Spain hewed most closely to the trajectory of more classic labor or green parties. By 2012 it had become clear that the Indignados could not maintain their momentum, and energies on the ground were dissipating. "The crisis is not enough," one activist admitted that year, disappointed by the protests' antipolitical stance. Without some minimal degree of institutional representation and leadership, the movement would fall prey to demagogues and cynics. It risked being dragged into the nationalist undertow already sweeping much of the West. Yet fresh waves of mobilization gathered force against evictions and renewed cuts to the public sector.[22] From 2012, a group of intellectuals, philosophers, and social scientists—sympathetic to the movement and historically in the radical left—began meeting weekly at Complutense University of Madrid. In March 2014, they founded a party with the aim of transferring the legacy of the Indignados into the field of institutional politics. Their inaugural campaign event took place in a former bus depot. When party cofounder and leader Pablo Iglesias spotted a crowd of supporters gathering outside, he stepped out with a megaphone in hand and joined their chant, echoing Barack Obama's slogan first adapted from the United Farm Workers: "¡Sí se puede!"

Partly thanks to Iglesias's skillful use of televised media, Podemos (We Can) secured 8 percent in the May 2014 European elections and nearly 21 percent in the 2015 general election. After a series of internal disputes and splits, the party fell to 13 percent in November 2019, running this time under the electoral alliance Unidas Podemos. It nonetheless entered a coalition government with Pedro Sánchez's Spanish Socialist Workers' Party (PSOE) and several regionalist parties. Iglesias became deputy prime minister and minister for social rights. After his withdrawal from active politics in 2021, the popular labor minister Yolanda Díaz emerged as the central figure of the Spanish left. In 2023 she founded Sumar (Add Up), a broad left platform. The governing coalition navigated the pandemic with relative success and was credited with an unorthodox but effective response to inflation. Yet after heavy defeats for PSOE and Sumar in regional and municipal elections in May 2023, amid gains by the conservative Partido Popular and the far-right Vox, Sánchez called snap national elections for July. In those, the Partido Popular overtook PSOE, with Vox narrowly ahead of Sumar for third place.

Italy's Movimento 5 Stelle showed itself more consistent than any other antipolitical movement in embracing digital tools as a means of addressing the question of institutionalization. Grillo, who consistently stressed that his movement/party was "neither left nor right," sought, alongside the late Gianroberto Casaleggio and his son Davide, to promote online participation. They developed the Rousseau platform, where supporters could debate political proposals and vote on the party's program in a spirit of grassroots democracy. Yet M5S rank and file quickly discovered that the agenda was largely set by a small inner circle, if not by Grillo himself: when two politicians proposed a loosening of immigration laws, they were publicly reprimanded by Grillo, despite a majority of members having voted in favor.[23]

At the polls, however, M5S enjoyed considerable success from the outset. In its first national contest in 2013, it came first with nearly 26 percent of the vote. In 2018, it climbed to 33 percent. After protracted coalition talks, liberal commentators' worst fears were realized: M5S entered a government with Matteo

Salvini's right-populist Lega, and the law professor Giuseppe Conte was appointed prime minister. Salvini, a bold tactician who never shied from provocation, steadily outmaneuvered M5S, becoming Italy's most popular politician—only to miscalculate by bringing down the coalition over a trivial issue. Conte managed to reconstitute a governing alliance and remain in office, but in 2021 President Sergio Mattarella installed former Goldman Sachs banker and ECB president Mario Draghi as head of a technocratic national unity government.

By the 2023 elections, M5S had collapsed to just 15 percent. Meloni, leader of the victorious Fratelli d'Italia, assumed office as prime minister in coalition with Salvini's Lega and Berlusconi's Forza Italia. For a time Grillo had ridden the wave of antipolitics with great success, but he ultimately fell victim to the volatile hyperpolitics that followed. The Movimento 5 Stelle failed to build a durable base or meaningful local and regional structures. Observers described it as a deliberately "skeletal" organization, whereas Salvini had access to an established network in the Lega's northern strongholds, and Meloni could draw on the organizational infrastructure of the old Movimento Sociale Italiano.[24] M5S, founded in a spirit of antipolitics, became a vehicle for the careers of political professionals like Conte. Another of its figureheads, Luigi Di Maio, published a book in 2021 titled *Un amore chiamato politica*—"A love affair called politics." A movement that had sought to rally all Italians under its banner now rallied virtually none.

After the momentum of Occupy and the British student movements dissipated, both the US and UK took unexpected turns in 2015. That April, Bernie Sanders announced his candidacy for the Democratic presidential nomination, challenging the presumptive favorite Hillary Clinton; a few weeks later, Jeremy Corbyn entered the race for Labour Party leader. The amorphous early phase of antipolitics now gave way to a period of semi-institutionalization, as two figures within established parties attempted to harness their energies for a kind of populist coup. Tellingly, both were white, decidedly old-fashioned, and well past retirement age. Born in 1949, Corbyn was only slightly younger than Sanders. Both men were veterans of the mass-political era. As their parties swung to the neoliberal center after 1989, the two spent the postpolitical ice age on the margins, Corbyn as a notoriously stubborn backbencher, Sanders as an independent Senator from Vermont, having left the House of Representatives in 2006. Where Clinton and Blair had squandered credibility with their centrist programs, these two set out—buoyed by mobilized millennials—to take over their parties and win back the estranged working class.

Even as Sanders, like Tsipras, rose to become a left-wing figure of hope—winning a devoted global following of young supporters ("Feel the Bern!")—he was ultimately defeated by Clinton, who in turn lost to Donald Trump in November 2016. Corbyn, by contrast, accomplished what had seemed impossible: in September 2015, he was elected leader of the Labour Party with 60 percent of the vote. Ironically, he benefited from a change to the party statutes introduced by his predecessor Ed Miliband, a relevant fact for what it reveals about the fate of mass parties and the deinstitutionalization of political participation. In an effort to weaken the unions, Miliband had opened up internal elections to so-called three-quid supporters in 2014. Anyone who affirmed support for Labour's values and paid a symbolic £3 fee could vote in party elections without becoming a full member (the block votes of affiliated unions were abolished at the same time). Miliband thus lowered the barriers to party entry, making it comparatively easy for Corbyn to seize control from within. Organized by campaigning groups such as Momentum, Corbyn's supporters signed up *en masse* as three-quid affiliates and delivered him the leadership.[25] The party also experienced a dramatic surge in full membership, rising from 190,000 in May 2015 to 515,000 just over a year later.[26]

Against the odds, Corbyn ran an insurgent campaign that brought Labour close to victory in the 2017 general election; he narrowly lost to incumbent Theresa May, who herself was forced into a coalition with the Democratic Unionist Party after losing her majority. Yet Corbyn's star fell almost as swiftly as it had risen. The indecisiveness in the Brexit saga cost him dearly, and in the 2019 election Labour suffered a historic defeat at the hands of Boris Johnson's Conservatives. Corbyn resigned and was succeeded by the right-wing Labour MP and former director of public prosecutions Keir Starmer, under whom membership has fallen by nearly half since its Corbyn-era peak.

That leaves the American Tea Party as the last of the antipolitical currents cited above. Once the Republicans captured the House of Representatives in the 2010 midterm elections, enabling them to obstruct much of President Obama's legislative agenda, the movement soon deserted the streets. According to Nils Kumkar, while the Tea Party remained "a kind of brand in internal party conflicts," it never regained its former momentum "on the ground" following the near-default crisis of 2011.[27] Meanwhile, however, a cohort of Tea Party candidates began making its way through the institutions. They would go on to become key supporters of Trump, who absorbed much of their libertarian-conservative program. In this sense, the Tea Party proved the most successful of the movements examined here. Occupy initially dissipated, only to be partially reactivated by Sanders before he was outmaneuvered by a centrist rival. Syriza has since entered decline; Greece's conservatives now have a firmer hold on power than at any point in recent years and could, if necessary, form alliances further to the right. A similar trajectory may be underway in Spain. Italy's Movimento 5 Stelle has marginalized itself. In German federal elections held in early 2025, Sahra Wagenknecht's left-populist BSW narrowly fell short of the 5 percent threshold to form a parliamentary group. Corbyn suffered a crushing defeat at the hands of Johnson's Tories, and Starmer's premiership has seen Labour return firmly to the center-right fold.

Viewed from the left, the balance sheet of roughly fifteen years of antipolitics is sobering.[28] At the beginning of 2019, Houellebecq, ever attuned to the spirit of the age, paid tribute to the greatest of all antipoliticians in a *Harper's* essay titled "Donald Trump Is a Good President."[29] The novelist justified this verdict with reference to Trump's nationalism, his supposed rejection of interventionist foreign policy, shared hostility to the EU, and his willingness to break with free-trade orthodoxy. On the whole, Houellebecq congratulated the American people: "They did well to elect a president with roots in what is sometimes called 'civil society.'"

As for the schema traced here, however, the Tea Party's relative success—especially when contrasted with the left-wing movements that emerged around the same time—retains significance for another reason. Might it bear on the earlier question, raised in connection with Trump and fascism, of whether the right wing of the political spectrum has been more effective than the left in generating new forms of social capital, or at least preserving what remains? Would this allow the conservative petty bourgeoisie in rural areas to translate their anger more effectively into politics, and eventually into policy?

At this point, the previously mentioned distinction between the conservative base and capitalist elites acquires its saliency. In the case of the Tea Party, there has been sustained debate over whether it ever constituted a genuine grassroots insurgency. Some writers reject the label altogether, invoking the term "astroturfing" and arguing that the Tea Party was less a spontaneous popular uprising than the long-prepared project of libertarian think tanks and billionaire donors.[30] It was, on this view, strategically orchestrated to furnish the Republican Party and its backers with shock troops in their struggle against the Democrats. From this perspective, the movement was never grounded in authentic or sustained civil society mobilization.

Theda Skocpol, however, disputes said interpretation. Although it is true that conservative organizations eventually climbed aboard and media outlets such as Fox News helped to manufacture the Tea Party's mystique, she argues that reducing the phenomenon to "top-down maneuvers" misses the point. "Ordinary conservative citizens and community activists, almost all white and mostly older," she writes, "provided angry passion and volunteered their energies to make the early Tea Party more than just occasional televised rallies."

> Local Tea Party groups met in churches, libraries, and restaurants, and collected small contributions or sold books, pins, bumper stickers, and other Tea Party paraphernalia on commission to cover their modest costs. They did not get by on checks from the Koch brothers or any other wealthy advocacy organizations.[31]

No matter how the relative weight of bottom-up versus top-down dynamics are calculated, the fact remains that the right was here better positioned than the left, both on the ground and among elite actors.

Two further elements must be considered when accounting for the success of the right's variety of antipolitics. The model of neo-Bonapartist acclamation, whereby figures like Trump or Salvini bypass established institutions and procedures to rile up their supporters—often through transgressive tweets and Facebook posts—without requiring them to join parties or help shape coherent agendas, is plainly well-suited to the current institutional and media environment. Whether their voters spend most of their time living in atomized isolation, like Marx's proverbial potatoes, is ultimately of little concern to the right's leadership. The left, by contrast, depends more heavily on mobilization and sustained participation—as Engels previously put it, workers "cannot do without a strong organization, well-defined by rules," and left-wing parties require what Gramsci called "a collective will, which has already been recognized and has to some extent asserted itself in action."

This renders the task of left-wing antipolitical actors—Sanders, Corbyn, Tsipras, Iglesias—considerably more difficult. In the twenty-first century, they can no longer rely solely on the working class but must instead unify divergent, loosely left-aligned class fractions: politicized millennials, segments of the new petty bourgeoisie, ideally even some conservative-leaning milieus, united under a hegemonic project.

Here, theoretical support could be drawn from figures such as Chantal Mouffe and Ernesto Laclau, who, starting in the early 1980s, urged the construction of "chains of equivalence" between diverse social groups.[32] Laclau in particular—who before his death in 2014 had lent his support to Hugo Chávez in Venezuela and to the Kirchners in Argentina—became a kind of posthumous prophet for Syriza, Podemos, Corbyn's Labour Party, and Jean-Luc Mélenchon's La France Insoumise. The idea of juxtaposing the people against a governing caste, so frequently invoked in this milieu, was drawn directly from Laclau and Mouffe. Left antipolitics, on their reading, had to build heterogeneous alliances and traverse class boundaries.[33] Was this the arc through which postpolitics might surpass antipolitics to rediscover classical politics, suitably updated?

Iglesias's close collaborator Íñigo Errejón, long regarded as Podemos's chief strategist, repeatedly insisted that they were operating, like the Movimento 5 Stelle, "beyond left and right."[34] Mélenchon campaigned under the slogan "*Fâchés, mais pas fachos*"—"angry, but not fascist." Yet such overtures to conservative constituencies, in particular former industrial workers, risked alienating another crucial and highly mobilized part of the left's prospective alliance: educated, networked, cosmopolitan millennials. Corbyn's fate was emblematic. His ambiguous stance on Brexit stemmed, in part, from the need to reconcile two competing constituencies: on the one hand, the Euroskeptic working-class Labour base in England's former "Red Wall"; on the other, Labour's young, overwhelmingly pro-European supporters in London and the Momentum milieu. The institutional challenge of the 2010s—how to mobilize effectively in an era of deinstitutionalization—was then overlaid by an older social-democratic dilemma: should the left focus exclusively on its core working-class constituency or attempt to unify disparate strata from both the old and new middle classes?

By the end of the 2010s, the right had seemingly taken the lead in the race to end the postpolitical era. Brexit, the election of Trump, and the rise of Salvini, Marine Le Pen, Viktor Orbán, and Germany's AfD all testified to this without ambiguity. It was also the moment when Tillmans began campaigning for Britain to remain in the EU. In a sense, one might say that it was the success of right-wing antipolitics that gave birth to hyperpolitics.

In the years after 2008, this repoliticization was largely confined to specific subsections of society: the traditional conservative petty bourgeoisie and frustrated, downwardly mobile millennials. But now the formerly passive, postpolitical liberal center underwent a kind of reactive shock-politicization. In parallel, movements like #MeToo and Black Lives Matter showed that the demands of groups long marginalized under mass democracy had reached a tipping point. Women, people of color, and migrants could no longer be ignored. As history returned in the form of a global pandemic and inflation was triggered by Russia's invasion of Ukraine—forcing governments once more to intervene directly in the lives of their citizens—OECD countries found themselves engulfed in a kind of permanent Dreyfus Affair, one that extended to family gatherings, circles of friends, and workplace cliques.

In chapter 1, a four-quadrant schema was proposed for mapping the political forms examined in this book, structured along two axes: levels of politicization and the degree to which civil society networks and large membership-based organizations

Figure 3: Four forms of politics

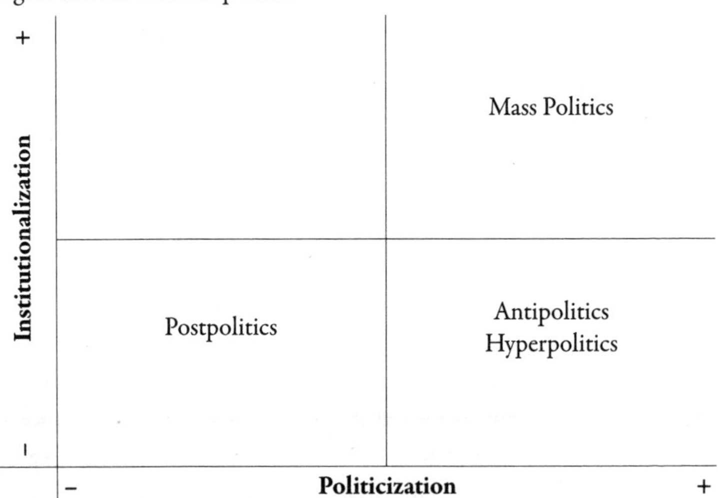

facilitate institutional political participation. Mass politics, conceived of as an ideal type, occupies the quadrant of high politicization and high institutionalization. Postpolitics, by contrast, is characterized by low politicization and low institutionalization. Antipolitics in turn signifies repoliticization under conditions of diminishing social capital and the continuing decline of unions and traditional parties.

It should by now be clear that hyperpolitics does not belong in the remaining quadrant—low politicization combined with high institutionalization (a space better suited to the second, more pacified phase of mass politics). In fact, hyperpolitics is situated in the same quadrant as antipolitics, though it diverges from the variant in several key respects. If antipolitics was initiated by social groups hit hard by the crisis of 2008, now the entirety of the public sphere is politicized. By the same token, while populism attached itself to a recognizable ideological vector, hyperpolitics is a permanently volatile, diffuse phenomenon. Whereas populist parties at least made the first steps towards reinstitutionalization, "hyperpolitical" refers to a general atmosphere rather than to specific actors. In this respect, hyperpolitics represents a redoubling of antipolitics, a mode of viral panic typical of the internet age with its short cycles of hype and outrage.

Visibly, the terrain of postpolitics shared many key features with the hyperpolitics that would finally come to supplant it: a demobilization and critical weakening of civil society, the hollowing out of parties, the increasing insulation of the state from popular pressure. Insofar as novelty invariably presupposes contrast, why not stick with a more familiar term?

In the years after the 2008 financial crash, the political ice age that had followed the collapse of the Berlin Wall began, steadily, to thaw as social movements once again raised the specter of interest bargaining and class conflict. Amid this populist awakening, organizational alternatives to the mass parties of old also sprouted up. Citizens enlisted in structures that permitted them to opt out of long-term, involuntary commitments, while politicians met less resistance at party congresses. The continuity with the preceding postpolitical era was clear: parties continued to hemorrhage members even as protest activity abounded.

Hyperpolitics, a curious admixture of old and new, ended the separation of public and private that had reigned since the post-political 1990s, but it did so on unfamiliar terms. Twentieth-century political movements, at least in their superpoliticized mode (defined at one extreme by fascism), spelled an end to the public-private divide instituted in the bourgeois nineteenth century. Political life has not reverted to this precedent. Instead, the mood of contemporary politics is one of incessant yet uncoordinated excitation. Emotionally, it is related to the crisis of attention characteristic of the age of the smartphone. "Hyper" indicates both supersession and intensification, the elongation of a vowel that has already been vocalized but does not yet spell out a new word.

This is not simply about securing a sense of continuity with the preceding period of postpolitics, which first split politics from policy, a gulf that hyperpolitics widens rather than bridges. From 2020 onward, millions marched against police violence, COVID policy, and climate inaction, making strident demands of their governments. In terms of turnout, these new movements could be impressive, and many of them effected remarkable changes in public opinion. Racial attitudes, for instance, have altered strikingly over the past decade, and genuflections to climate action are ubiquitous. A return to class themes is visible in productions such as the novels of Eribon's protégé Edouard Louis, Piketty's wildly popular economic history, and the Western enthusiasm for the Korean film *Parasite*, albeit in an individualistic, culturalist register.

On the policy front, however, achievements have been painfully ephemeral. Nor is this judgment limited to the left. On the right too, movements from the Tea Party to Stop the Steal flower and wilt with unnerving rapidity. Rather than concrete results, what all these political objects share is the ability to reproduce frenetic activity, relayed by an increasingly digital public sphere. Hyperpolitics bursts forth periodically only to recede, less a corrective to postpolitics than yet another manifestation.

4

Escape Routes

> Closing down, closing down! It's the end-of-the century sale. Everything must go! Modernity is over (without ever having happened), the orgy is over, the party is over—the sales are starting . . . We have lost history and have also, as a result, lost the end of history. We are laboring under the illusion of the end.[1]

As the 1990s drew to a close, Jean Baudrillard devoted a series of essays to the post-historical condition with titles both clairvoyant and metaphorical, including *The Illusion of the End* and *The Strike of Events*, source of the above epigraph.

The quote already bore the weight of retrospection. Baudrillard looked back on the decade after the "end of history" and now dismissed Fukuyama's pronouncement as premature. "The last great 'historic' event—the fall of the Berlin Wall," he wrote at the turn of the millennium, "signified something closer to an enormous repentance on the part of history." "Instead of seeking fresh perspectives, history appears rather to be splintering into scattered fragments, and phases of events and conflicts we had thought long gone are being reactivated."[2] What Baudrillard had in mind were not merely the remnants of modernity but elements older than modernity itself, returning to haunt the present, like the computer-generated dinosaurs in Steven Spielberg's *Jurassic Park* (1993), who in the film's closing scene crash into a museum and destroy the remains of their extinct kin. "Today," Baudrillard concluded, "we are caught as a species in a similar impasse, trapped between our fossils and our clones."[3] Another quarter-century on, his events and conflicts from the age of industrial modernity appear to be resurfacing, consistently with the question of whether they return only as disembedded virtual phantoms—or whether this time history is truly returning, dispelling the illusion of politics' demise.

The previous chapters traced a typology of political forms, framed on one end by the mass politics of the short twentieth century. Max Weber's "slow boring" died a gradual death during the inflation-ridden 1970s, succeeded by the privatized postpolitics of the long 1990s, whose atmospherics were captured by Putnam, Tillmans, and Ernaux. After 2008, this configuration was shaken by the antipolitical movements of the 2010s. Midway through the populist decade, antipolitics mutated into what was here termed hyperpolitics.

The latter's effects can now be observed across the ideological spectrum. On the surface, for instance, the Black Lives Matter protests would seem to have little in common with the mob that stormed the Capitol in January 2021. Morally, they are worlds apart—one protesting racism and police brutality, the other enthralled by conspiracy theories and the myth of a stolen election. Organizationally, however, these movements exhibit a striking set of similarities: fleeting in duration, they maintain no membership rolls and struggle to impose any real discipline on their adherents.

Political theorist Paolo Gerbaudo, drawing on Gilles Deleuze and Félix Guattari, has similarly described these new phenomena as "bodies without organs"—concentrated and muscular, yet without an internal metabolism.[4] Works such as Elias Canetti's *Crowds and Power* mark out the difference. Canetti, who began writing his classic text in interwar Vienna, was responding to the great strikes and demonstrations of the 1920s. The socialist militancy of those years provoked a violent reaction from the right; the period culminated in two organized mass movements confronting each other in parliaments and in the streets.

BLM demonstrators, climate strikers, and antilockdown protesters resemble less a militant collective than the aforementioned swarms, a myriad animated by brief, potent stimuli, stirred to action by charismatic influencers and digital demagogues. Anyone can join a Telegram channel or be invited to a group chat; the price of membership is low, the costs of exit even lower. Leaders can, of course, try to choreograph these broods—with social media posts of their own, television appearances, or "anti-disinformation" campaigns. But such choreography is no substitute for durable organization.

Hyperpolitics is the product of a hard but hollow environment, an attempt to break the iron grip of neoliberalism without the requisite tools to do so. The neoliberal state began as an interventionist experiment to shield the market from mass democracy—that was its avowedly hard side. To achieve this, however, it had to sever the party ties that bound it to popular constituencies, with all the obligations that entailed. In its mass-political phase, party democracy acted as a brake on capital accumulation. The response was to hollow said parties out and to transform the state from an active agent into an impartial arbiter.

That humanity faces world-historical challenges at the beginning of the twenty-first century—from global warming and economic inequality to mounting geopolitical tensions—is a banausic truism. The uprisings of the anti- and hyperpolitical era indicate at least a diffuse social consciousness of this fact. So far, however, their record has been meager. Is the global banking sector more tightly regulated than it was in 2008? The collapses of Silicon Valley Bank and the Credit Suisse crisis give reason to doubt it. In Britain, both Brexiteers and Corbynists promised increased funding for the National Health Service; the end of the pandemic found the NHS in its deepest crisis yet. Ambulances queue outside hospitals for want of beds and space in emergency rooms. The United States remains the only advanced industrial nation without a public health system. In Greece, the austerity policies imposed by the institutions were never fully lifted. The Movimento 5 Stelle did manage to introduce a rudimentary version of a universal basic income, after which Giorgia Meloni's right-wing government has vowed to dismantle it. All OECD nations are well short of meeting their climate goals.

Undoubtedly, this pattern shows variation on the organizational asymmetry mentioned before. Although some of the right's more extravagant promises were not fulfilled (the wall along the Mexican border, "Singapore-on-Thames"), Trump delivered his tax cuts, the UK left the European Union, Italy has moved toward a flat tax, and the EU's external borders are becoming ever more heavily militarized. By comparison, the left's hyperpolitical mobilization detonates like a neutron bomb: a moment ago, thousands of people were protesting in a square—now they have vanished, with the assailed power infrastructure intact.

The acephalous nature of left-wing hyperpolitics finds its most acute illustration in the Black Lives Matter demonstrations that brought millions of American citizens to the streets in the early months of the COVID pandemic. The protests took aim at systemic racism, police violence, and the sprawling surveillance and prison complex. Its targets were easy to discern: the US has the highest incarceration rate in the world, with 629 prison inmates per 100,000 inhabitants; in Russia, the figure in September 2022 was 324, in Germany just 67. In total, over 2 million people are incarcerated in American prisons—a figure surpassed only by the Soviet Union under Stalin. Enforcement is notoriously violent, and a central demand of the movement was to defund the police. Before the summer of 2020, the rallying point of the US left was Bernie Sanders's campaign for the Democratic presidential nomination, a belated sequel to the antipolitical revolts that broke out after 2008. Whatever their horizontalist ideals, they demanded remedies for debt dependency, income inequality, and the decades-long degradation of social welfare provisions. Sanders built on this momentum, advocating lower university tuition fees, higher taxes on corporations and capital gains, and the introduction of a public healthcare system.

Historians have long argued that there is a close connection between the underdevelopment of the American welfare state and the overdevelopment of its carceral counterpart.[5] The US labor movement, as noted, was never as strong as its European equivalents. Nor was the indigenous bourgeoisie discredited by collaboration with fascism after the Second World War. On the contrary, it confidently presided over an expanding economic empire that extended its reach into Europe and the Pacific. American capitalists were thus able to roll back many of the limited social achievements of the New Deal, prioritizing the Cold War arms buildup and fillips to consumer spending.

Meanwhile, Southern sharecropping entered into crisis under the pressure of increasing mechanization. Black Americans, who had previously worked small plots of land as tenant farmers, migrated to the industrial regions of the North. There, automation and early deindustrialization meant that by the 1960s, factories could no longer absorb the growing surplus of labor—and in times of recession, black workers were the first to be let go, on the principle "last hired, first fired." The resulting lack of economic prospects led, as John Clegg and Adaner Usmani have argued, to an increase in violence and crime.[6] The state subsequently faced two options. It could pursue social reforms, redistribute wealth downward, and support impoverished urban centers. Given the chronic weakness of the American working class, this path was not pursued. Instead, authorities elected to address the problem "on the cheap," through mass incarceration and the construction of a vast prison-industrial complex in lieu of expansive welfare institutions.

Against this politico-economic backdrop, demands to resolve systemic problems simply by defunding the police will appear painfully limited. To adapt Weber's apothegm, the conception of politics they disclose more closely resembles a laser cutting through Styrofoam than a drill biting into resistant timber. As they note, US criminal justice system is in urgent need of reform—more humane prison conditions, shorter sentences, and the decriminalization of minor offenses. But if the situation is to be fundamentally altered, as Clegg and Usmani argue, what is required is the construction of a mature welfare state and its concomitant set of social rights, and the first step in that direction is to force the ruling elites to accept a redistribution of resources:

> If we are right that the overdevelopment of the American penal state is a symptom of the underdevelopment of the American social policy, meaningful reform is in large part the task of winning redistribution from ruling elites. It will be costly. And there will thus be losers, who will resist it. The end of American mass incarceration is not a technical problem for

> which there are smart, straightforward, but just not-yet-realized solutions. Rather, it is a political problem, the solution of which will require confronting the entrenched power of the wealthy. In this sense, the task before us is to build the capacities of poor and working-class Americans to win redress from their exploiters.[7]

The George Floyd Justice in Policing Act, introduced by Democratic Congress members in February 2021 in response to the Black Lives Matter protests, stalled due to Republican resistance in the Senate. In October 2021, the *New York Times* reported that many police departments that experienced post-2020 cuts had seen their previous budgets restored or even increased. Police brutality has continued to rise in the interim.[8] According to the Mapping Police Violence project, US law enforcement officers killed 1,200 people in 2022.[9] It was the highest recorded tally since the organization began collecting data, and it continued to rise in 2023 and 2024.

In September 1957, a shipwreck southwest of the Azores kept the German reading public in suspense for days. On August 11, the *Pamir*—a four-masted barque usually deployed as a trainee ship—set sail from Buenos Aires with almost 4,000 tons of barley on board, bound for Hamburg. On the morning of September 21, the ship sent out its SOS calls, but contact was lost around midday. No trace of its eighty-six crew members could be found, including several young cadets. Two days later, as part of an international search operation, an American steamer retrieved a damaged lifeboat with five survivors; within forty-eight hours, another sailor was rescued alive. Investigations revealed that a severe hurricane had crossed the Atlantic at the time of the disaster—a ship with the *Pamir*'s design should have been able to withstand such a storm, yet a fatal mistake had been made when loading the vessel due to time pressure: instead of stowing the barley in sacks in the barque's hull as usual, the grain had been poured in without prior packaging. As barley has a particularly high flow velocity, the cargo shifted uncontrollably from side to side when the *Pamir* was caught in the storm in front of the Azores. Incapable of reequilibrating, the ship capsized and eventually sank. No other survivors were located.

Returning to Sloterdijk's nautical metaphors, it is the *Pamir*, rather than the superferry, that offers a fitting emblem for the hyperpolitical present. In earlier times, individuals were embedded in dense social networks and participated in a wide array of intermediate associations. Today's societies are composed of increasingly atomized and isolated individuals. As long as history moves along smoothly and predictably, this need not necessarily be a problem. But when societies enter choppier waters, atomization amplifies their volatility—and the collective incapacity to respond to today's political and ecological crises.

The corrective to our hyperpolitical impasse, implicit throughout the foregoing chapters, of drawing atomized individuals back into parties and unions may seem nostalgic, authoritarian, or simply unrealistic. Rightly so, perhaps. As the sociologist Ingolfur Blühdorn notes, Westerners emancipated themselves twice: first from traditional authorities, then from the kind of political commitment required to accomplish that emancipation.[10] Who could command them to reverse course? To extend Baudrillard's simile, recreating the mass party of the industrial age might be likened to the genomic reconstruction of a mammoth from DNA samples extracted out of the Siberian permafrost—a scientifically interesting but practically pointless exercise. Even the most hardened reactionary must accept by now that no amount of railing against the legacy of 1968 and postmodern hedonism will inspire the youth to unplug their consoles and start attending church in formal wear on Sunday. Similarly, anyone who imagined that the Russian invasion of Ukraine might augur a renaissance of martial vigor in the West—young men and women flocking to recruiting offices—was quickly disabused. Military spending may be on the rise across NATO states, British journalist Anatol Lieven dryly observed in early 2022, but anyone expecting the revival of Prussian militarism at the heart of Europe had clearly "never been to a German disco."[11]

Another creature from the twentieth century that has begun once again to stretch out its claws also appears to be a grin without a cat. After an era of postpolitical stability blessed with steady prices and wage restraint, the pandemic triggered a surge of sector-specific inflation, which escalated after the outbreak of war in Ukraine and spilled over into other areas of the economy. Warnings of a wage–price spiral were soon revived, and central banks responded with sharp hikes in interest rates. Most episodes of inflation in the twentieth century, however, resulted at least in part from collective wage demands. Inflation was therefore not merely a technical datum but an index of *history*: the moment that a factor of production, labor, became a political actor with a claim to its share of the collectively generated surplus. It was precisely this metamorphosis that neoliberalism set out to reverse.

With the consequent fissiparation of the workers' movement, such pressures dwindled. The Great Resignation galvanized by American and EU stimulus checks yielded a politics of radical exit, not voice—strike activity has seldom been lower, and ours is still "an era of spectacularly lopsided class power," in the words of Adam Tooze.[12] "The working class as a cohesive social force no longer exists," the *Financial Times* reported in 2022. "Businesses can safely protect their margins and the burden of inflation will fall on labour as real wages fall."[13] If class struggle is indeed the motor of history, and if strong trade unions generated the cost-push cycles of past decades, the resurgence of inflation should signal that the engine is running again. But the contemporary macrodata scarcely bear this out. Contemporary inflation is driven by the vagaries of a leaderless and anarchic world economy, where modest wage gains can easily be offset by ballooning costs and energy prices.

For the left to catch up with its rivals will require a philosophical reckoning with the historic decomposition of voluntary association dissected in these pages. Possibly, though, the adjective "voluntary" indicates a deeper epistemological obstacle. Did people in the past truly join unions, parties, and religious associations voluntarily, in the same way that a Houellebecq protagonist picks an exotic vacation package from a catalogue? As casually as one signs up for a gym membership? Or did they do so simply because it was customary—in their milieu, their family, their workplace—and because their fathers and grandmothers had done so before them? A matter of free choice or institutional inertia?

It is worth revisiting the immersive character of political belonging, including the passions it once aroused, in this "Age of Extremes." In his memoir *Interesting Times*, Eric Hobsbawm recalls "the last legal demonstration" of the Communist Party of Germany, held on January 25, 1933. In response to a procession by the Nazi Sturmabteilung the Party had organized a "mass march through the dusky streets of Berlin" to KPD headquarters on what is now Rosa-Luxemburg-Platz. Hobsbawm took part, "probably with some comrades from the SSB [Sozialistischer Schutzbund], even if I can't remember them individually." The event proved unforgettable for the historian, who seventy years later could still summon the atmosphere:

Next to sex, the activity combining bodily experience and intense emotion to the highest degree is the participation in a mass demonstration at a time of great public exaltation. Unlike sex, which is essentially individual, it is by its nature collective, and unlike the sexual climax, at any rate for men, it can be prolonged for hours. On the other hand, like sex it implies some physical action—marching, chanting slogans, singing—through which the merger of the individual in the mass, which is the essence of the collective experience, finds expression. The occasion has remained unforgettable, although I can recall no details of this demonstration. I can only remember endless hours of marching, or rather alternately shuffling and waiting, in the freezing cold—Berlin winters are hard—between shadowy buildings (and policemen?) along the dark wintry streets. I cannot remember red flags and slogans, but if there were any—and there must have been some—they were lost in the grey mass of the marchers. What I can remember is singing, with intervals of heavy silence. We sang—I still have the tattered pamphlet with the texts of the songs, ticks against my favourites: the "Internationale"; the peasant war song "Des Geyers schwarzer Haufen"; the sentimental graveyard doggerel of "Der kleine Trompeter," which (I am told) the leader of the GDR, Erich Honecker, wanted played at his funeral; "Dem Morgenrot entgegen," the Soviet Red Airmen's Song; Hanns Eisler's "Der rote Wedding"; and the slow, solemn, hieratic "Brüder, zur Sonne, zur Freiheit." We belonged together. I returned home to Halensee as if in a trance. When, in British isolation two years later, I reflected on the basis of my communism, this sense of "mass ecstasy" (*Massenekstase*, for I wrote my diary in German) was one of the five components of it—together with pity for the exploited, the aesthetic appeal of a perfect and comprehensive intellectual system, "dialectical

> materialism," a little bit of the Blakean vision of the new Jerusalem and a good deal of intellectual anti-philistinism. But in January 1933 I did not analyse my convictions. Five days later Hitler was appointed Chancellor.[14]

It is reasonable to assume that people joining a Fridays for Future rally, or participants in Black Lives Matter demonstrations, have kindred trance-like experiences; one finds loudspeaker trucks, possibly someone is playing music from an iPhone over a Bluetooth speaker. And yet the mass march described by Hobsbawm nonetheless took place in a completely different environment. The then fifteen-year-old had not joined the march to Rosa-Luxemburg-Platz on his own but did so together with comrades from the SSB, a Communist-linked paramilitary organization. A Party representative had selected songs for the occasion, printed, and disseminated them. Reading the (auto)biographies of German socialists of Hobsbawm's generation, such as the aforementioned Wolfgang Abendroth or Comintern valkyrie Olga Benario, it is striking how much time, energy, and creativity they devoted to building class consciousness and organizing their fellow students, neighbors, and coworkers.

Membership in these groups must have seemed far more self-evident to contemporaries than it does today. No wonder, since large and powerful institutions like the military, heavy industry, and the Church were still inseparably woven into everyday life. Until the 1980s, socialists faced societies in which the primary form of sociability was religious. Gáspár Miklós Tamás draws out the parallel in a remarkable passage:

> A Hungarian sociological survey from 1906 shows that a working-class housing estate in Transylvania has one portrait

> of Marx and one of Lassalle per flat, workers are teetotal in a heavily drinking society, and open atheists and anticlericalists in a polity dominated by the church militant; church weddings are frowned upon, there are attempts at a healthy diet, non-competitive sports (not shared with outsiders) are encouraged (in Central Europe there were special socialist workers' athletic championships and mass musical choir contests until 1945); non-socialist charities are rejected, parties are held only in daylight to avoid immorality, and at least the men are trying—in a country of barefoot illiterates one generation away from the village primeval—to read social science and serious history. Admirable as this is, it must have been, for all intents and purposes, *a sect.*[15]

The decline of this counter-power went hand in hand with socio-geographic changes in the structure of working life. As Vivek Chibber writes, "the physical layout of large industrial centers" pushed "workers together into crowded spaces" while "separating them from their employers."[16] When industry abandoned cities and working-class families relocated to newly built suburbs, the shift had far-reaching effects on class identity, laying the groundwork for what Marx had described as "potato sack politics." As Hobsbawm himself recorded, "urban development, public and private, was destroying the very bases which had allowed the formation of the 'urban villages' on which so much of labour strength had rested." "The effect of all this on labour movements," he wrote in the late 1980s, "has been to deprive them of their former cohesion."[17]

The patrilineal element underlying that bygone cohesiveness should not be discounted either. Tamás's parents were Communists; his Jewish mother only escaped deportation to Auschwitz because, as a Bolshevik, she was already in prison. Disillusioned by postwar Stalinization, his parents nonetheless remained staunch party loyalists. As a teenager, Tamás later recounted,

> When my father was thoroughly disenchanted with the system, I asked him why he still called himself a Communist. He showed me a little plastic—well, I suppose, bakelite—cube, with six little photos glued on its sides: the portraits of some of the best friends of his youth, tortured to death by the royal Hungarian and Romanian secret services, or by the Gestapo in that awful year, 1944. "Because I cannot explain it to them," he said.[18]

Without a reinstitutionalization of political engagement, the left will remain hostage to impotent volatility, and its adversaries will continue to enjoy a decisive advantage. At the same time, the present is worlds away from the institutional landscape of the interwar period or the organized capitalism of the post-1945 era. Today's impasse can hardly be undone by a voluntaristic act of will, simply because a young Belgian historian exhorts citizens to join a local party branch or take out a union card. This raises the question of whether the mass-political dynamism of what is in retrospect an idealized golden age of social democracy was not in fact a contingent product of specific social conditions. Before the dawn of modernity, societies were perhaps so totally institutionalized—through feudal structures, religion, tradition, guild regulations, and so on—that there was no space for political agency in the modern sense. Then, this conventional narrative goes, came industrialization, urbanization, democratization, liberalization, educational expansion, and so forth, all contributing to the trends Putnam surveyed, down to our individualized and deinstitutionalized hyperpolitical present. It may be that only a specific sociological context offered the requisite conditions for effective collective action, made possible by the density of interpersonal bonds. "Whether we will or no, we are bundles of hyphens," wrote the English Fabian and sometime Labour leader Harold Laski in 1916, "for man is so essentially an associative animal that his nature is largely determined by the relationships thus formed."[19] In this optic, organizations of the working class could reach for a secure anthropological basis. Lenin's understanding of revolutionary class consciousness likewise assumed a nigh-irresistible drive toward association on the part of workers, who then had to be spurred beyond narrow corporatism by a revolutionary party. Today, Gopal Balakrishnan writes, "not even a spontaneous trade union consciousness can be assumed."[20]

Granting that barriers to sustained, institutionally oriented political participation are indeed higher today, the prospects for any renewal will have to be sought in everyday life—in those circumstances in which people still regularly enter into contact with others, in which common concerns are self-evident. Once these were to be found above all in the great factories and construction sites of the industrial age. The epochal decomposition of this world remains the starting point for left strategy in the twenty-first century. Presupposing its irrelevance, some have looked instead to the sphere of social reproduction or care work. In an era of precarious employment and working from home, many no longer interact with coworkers in person on a daily basis, one still has to drop their children at daycare, attend parent-teacher meetings, or visit their own parents in retirement homes. The average Western European today is more likely to interact with geriatric nurses than workplace union reps. The COVID-19 pandemic laid bare the devastating scars left by austerity policies in many of these facilities and the urgent need for a political response. Another suggested point of entry is then located at the street or neighborhood level, where the effects of gentrification and asset-price inflation can be witnessed first-hand, denying housing to whole layers of the population while a select few gorge on the fruits of property speculation. Campaigns like Deutsche Wohnen & Co. enteignen in Berlin or Barcelona en Comú, the municipal platform promoted by Mayor Ada Colau, at least show that there are quotidian opportunities around which more consequential forms of engagement might gradually crystallize.

Yet the spheres of production and distribution can hardly be written off that easily. The world of work remains the site where surplus value is produced and economic interests directly clash, whereas parents and tenants can only appeal to the fiscal state, which in turn depends on the willingness of capitalist elites to redistribute. It may be that, at a time when talk of reshoring, Green New Deals, and industrial policy is ubiquitous across the OECD zone, occasions conducive to longer-term mobilization will present themselves. Confronted with the continuing decline in unionization rates, rising precarity, and the increasingly divergent interests among different categories of workers, such a thought may seem naive. It cruelly recalls the old joke about the tourist couple who ask an Irish farmer how to get to Dublin; the farmer replies: "Well, I wouldn't start from here." Still, the journey will have to begin somewhere.

Postpolitics is over. The eschatological rumor that politics is dead, as Ernaux had it, has been disproven. For now, however, it is as if our patient has awoken from a coma to a state of frenzied activity, without ever coming to terms with the symptoms. The father of psychoanalysis knew the reflex all too well. What is distinctive about melancholy, Sigmund Freud observed, is its "tendency to turn into the symptomatically opposite state of mania," a "cyclical insanity" that leaves the patient prone to "the regular alternation of melancholic and manic phases," struggling in both cases to repair the loss of the libidinal object.[21] Freud's insight finds a late echo in the words of a Belgian photographer born in the mid-1990s:

> My generation constantly oscillates between the realization that we need to get moving, preferably very quickly, and the feeling that all is in vain. The true challenge—to change things—appears nigh impossible.[22]

Acknowledgments

This book's cover might carry a single name but nonetheless the book resists exclusive authorial claims. Most of the chapters were commissioned by friends with a better eye for compelling ideas: Ronan Burtenshaw (*Tribune*) and Bhaskar Sunkara (*Jacobin*). The first insisted that I turn a furtive tweet into a full-length essay; the second rightly believed that the left had something to learn from Robert Putnam. Afterward, Thomas Meaney insisted that the pieces in question did, in fact, add up to a book.

Most of the chapters were written in a toponymic sister town of Belgium: Ghent, upstate New York, during a three-week residency with Art Omi. My thanks go out to Karsten Kredel for arranging the residency, and Art Omi for its hospitality. Individual chapters drafted in Ghent found their way to magazines. The editors at *The Point*—Rachel Wiseman, Jon Baskin, Anastasia Berg—helped to finesse a sketch into an independent essay. Other interlocutors proved indispensable: Benjamin Fong, Oliver Eagleton, Dustin Guastella, John-Baptist Oduor, Alex Hochuli, Chris Crawford, Rudi Laermans, Grey Anderson, David Adler, Gautham Shiralagi, Dominik Leusder, Loren Balhorn, Daniel Zamora, Dries Daniëls, Arthur Borriello, Corey Robin, Caitlin Doherty, and Gerard-Jan Claes. It is difficult to imagine the book without Heinrich Geiselberger, who not only translated but also restructured initial drafts—*sine qua non*—which were here returned into an original Anglophone version.

Excerpts

Earlier versions of chapter 1 first appeared as essays in *Tribune* ("How the World Went from Post-Politics to Hyper-Politics," January 3, 2022'), the *Point* ("Everything Is Hyperpolitical," February 22, 2023), *Die Wochenzeitung* ("Hyperpolitik: Die neuen Aufstände jenseits von Nostalgie und Zukunftseuphorie," May 11, 2023), *Damage Magazine* ("It Might Take a While Before History Starts Again," March 25, 2020), and *New Left Review* ("Animatron," March 3, 2022). Versions of chapter 2 first appeared in *Jacobin* ("From Bowling Alone to Posting Alone," December 5, 2022). Parts of the fourth chapter first appeared as "The Illusion of the End" in the journal *New Perspectives* (published online on October 10, 2022), *New Statesman* ("G. M. Tamas: The Prophet of Post-Fascism," January 17, 2023), and *Damage Magazine* ("The Utopia We Deserve," July 5, 2023). The introduction appeared in *New Left Review* as "Hyperpolitics in America" (149: September–October 2024).

Notes

Preface: Hyperpolitics, USA

1. Jean Baudrillard, *America*, trans. Chris Turner (London: Verso, 1998; London: Verso, 2010), 126–8. Citations refer to 2010 edition.
2. Ibid., 126–7.
3. Matthew Karp, "Party and Class in American Politics," *New Left Review* II, no.139 (January–February 2023), 131–44.
4. Christian Lorentzen, "Not a Tough Crowd," *London Review of Books* 46, no. 17 (September 12, 2024).
5. Bill Clinton, "Remarks by the President at Presentation of the National Medal of the Arts and the National Humanities Medal," Washington DC, September 29, 1999.
6. Peter Mair, "Ruling the Void," *New Left Review* II, no. 42 (November–December 2006), 25–51, 25; citing E. E. Schattschneider, *The Semi-Sovereign People: A Realist's View of Democracy in America* (New York: Holt, Rinehart and Winston, 1960).
7. Perry Anderson, "US Elections: Testing Formula Two," *New Left Review* II, no. 8 (March–April 2001), 5–22, 15.
8. Perry Anderson, "Jottings on the Conjuncture," *New Left Review* II, no. 48 (November–December 2007), 5–37, 25.
9. According to the University of Florida's Election Lab dataset, available at election.lab.ufl.edu.

10. Friedrich Engels, 1891 postscript to Karl Marx, *The Civil War in France*.
11. Matt Karp, "The Politics of a Second Gilded Age," *Jacobin*, February 17, 2021.
12. Eric Hobsbawm, "The Machine Breakers," *Past and Present* 1, no. 1 (February 1952), 57–70, 59.
13. Martin Gilens, "Inequality and Democratic Responsiveness: Who Gets What They Want from Government?" *Princeton Government Working Papers*, 2004.
14. Karen Petrou, "Bidenomics Has a Mortal Enemy, and It Isn't Trump," *New York Times*, November 16, 2023.
15. Tim Barker, "False Hopes," *Sidecar*, September 27, 2024, newleftreview.org.
16. Lorentzen, "Not a Tough Crowd"; on the 2024 Democratic National Convention: "I have attended four previous political conventions and I have never witnessed a crowd so much in love with politicians or so ecstatic about expressing it."

1. A Grin Without a Cat

1. James Welling, "Bernd and Hilla Becher," ArtSeen, *Brooklyn Rail*, September 2022; available at brooklynrail.org.
2. Artspace Editors, "Wolfgang Tillmans Opens Up on His Art, His Influences, and His Personal Tragedy," *Artspace*, September 14, 2015.
3. Guy Debord, "Foreword to the Third French Edition of *The Society of the Spectacle*" (c. 1992); available at libcom.org.
4. Cited in Stathis Kouvelakis, "Syriza's Rise and Fall (Interview)," *New Left Review* II, no. 97 (January–February 2016), 45–70, 68.
5. Charles Maier, *The Project State and Its Rivals* (Cambridge, MA: Harvard University Press, 2023), 317.
6. Nicholas Gamso, *Art After Liberalism* (New York: Columbia University Press, 2022).
7. Jean Baudrillard, *Cool Memories*, trans. Chris Turner (London: Verso, 1990), 1: 223.

8. Ibid., 223–4.
9. David Campany, "Photography, Encore," in *Time Present: Photography from the Deutsche Bank Collection* (Frankfurt: Deutsche Bank, 2014).
10. Emily Witt, "The Life and Art of Wolfgang Tillmans," *New Yorker*, September 3, 2018.
11. Adam Tooze, "Manchmal muss man etwas wagen," interview by Mark Schieritz and Petra Pinzler, *Die Zeit*, July 6, 2023.
12. Roger L. Martin and Martin Reeves, "Strategy in a Hyperpolitical World," *Harvard Business Review*, November–December 2022.
13. Cited in Intelligencer Staff, "How We're Feeling as America's Moment of Truth Arrives," *New York Magazine*, November 3, 2020.
14. Max Weber, *Political Writings*, ed. Peter Lassman, trans. Ronald Speirs (Cambridge: Cambridge University Press, 1994), 369.
15. Annie Ernaux, *Les années* (Paris: Gallimard, 2008); *The Years*, trans. Alison L. Strayer (New York: Seven Stories Press, 2017), 144. Citations are to the English translation.
16. Ibid., 204, 231.
17. Michel Clouscard, *De la modernité, Rousseau ou Sartre: De la philosophie de la Révolution française au consensus de la contre-révolution libérale* (Paris: Messidor, 1985); Cornelius Castoriadis, *Une société à la dérive: Entretiens et débats, 1974–1997* (Paris: Seuil, 2005).
18. Sam Kriss, "The End of the End of the End," *First Things*, February 2022.
19. Mark Fisher, *Capitalism Realism: Is There No Alternative?* (London: John Hunt, 2022).
20. Peter Sloterdijk, *Im selben Boot: Versuch über die Hyperpolitik* (Frankfurt am Main: Suhrkamp, 1993), 12.
21. Ibid., 13, 25.
22. Ibid., 13, 32, 26.
23. Ibid., 49, 52, 59.
24. Ibid., 53, 59.
25. Ibid., 13f.

26. Ibid., 74f.
27. Ibid., 74f.
28. Michel Houellebecq, "Je ne crois pas aux déclarations du genre 'rien ne sera plus jamais comme avant,'" *France Culture*, May 4, 2020.
29. Christopher Caldwell, "A Bellow from France," *Commentary*, March 2020.

2. Putnam from the Left

1. Daniel A. Cox, "The State of American Friendship: Change, Challenges, and Loss," American Enterprise Institute, June 8, 2021; available at aei.org.
2. Vivek H. Murthy, "Surgeon General: We Have Become a Lonely Nation; It's Time to Fix That," *New York Times*, April 30, 2023.
3. "Loneliness in the EU: Insights from Survey and Online Media Data," JCR Science for Polity Report (Luxemburg: Publications Office of the European Union, 2021); available at publications.jrc.ec.europa.eu.
4. Jean-Claude Michéa, "À voix nue: La chance d'avoir des parents communistes," *France Culture*, January 7, 2019.
5. Christian Jambet and Guy Lardreau, *L'Ange: Pour une cynégétique du semblant* (Paris: Grasset, 1976), 137.
6. Michel Houellebecq, *Submission*, trans. Lorin Stein (New York: Farrar, Strauss and Giroux, 2015), 56–57.
7. Robert D. Putnam, *Bowling Alone: The Collapse and Revival of American Community* (New York: Simon & Schuster, 2000).
8. Ibid., 277–84.
9. Ibid., 281.
10. Ibid., 280.
11. Ibid., 284.
12. Ibid., 180.
13. Robert Putnam, "Afterword," in *Bowling Alone: The Collapse and Revival of American Community*, 2nd ed. (New York: Simon & Schuster, 2020), 415–46.

14. Melinda Cooper, *Family Values: Between Neoliberalism and the New Social Conservatism* (New York: Zone Books, 2017), 158.
15. Nancy Fraser, "Contradictions of Capital and Care," *New Left Review* II, no. 100 (July–August 2016), 99–117, 113.
16. Daniel Zamora, "Why Your Flights Keep Getting Cancelled," *New Statesman*, July 14, 2022.
17. "About Three-in-Ten US Adults Are Now Religiously Unaffiliated," Pew Research, December 14, 2021; available at pewresearch.org.
18. D. Clark, "Average Weekly Attendance for the Church of England from 2009 to 2021," Statista, December 7, 2022; available at statista .com.
19. Lorenzo Macchi, "Weekly Church Attendance in Italy, 2001–2024," Statista, June 19, 2025; available at statista.com.
20. Marc Tracy, "Voting Alone," *New York Times*, September 20, 2020.
21. Marie Jahoda, Paul F. Lazarsfeld, and Hans Zeisel, *Marienthal: The Sociography of an Unemployed Community* (New Brunswick, NJ: Transaction, 1971), 16.
22. G. M. Tamás, "Telling the Truth About Class," *Socialist Register* 42 (2006): 9.
23. Antonio Gramsci, *Selections from the Prison Notebooks*, ed. and trans. Quintin Hoare and Geoffrey Nowell Smith (New York: International Publishers, 1971), 129.
24. Cited in Renato Cristi, *Carl Schmitt and Authoritarian Liberalism: Strong State, Free Economy* (Cardiff: University of Wales Press, 1998), 219.
25. Didier Eribon, *Returning to Reims*, trans. Michael Lucey (New York: Semiotext(e), 2013), 125.
26. Ibid., 43.
27. Pier Palo Pasolini, "Il romanzo delle stragi," *Corriere della Sera*, November 14, 1974.
28. Wolfgang Abendroth, *Ein Leben in der Arbeiterbewegung: Gespräche*, ed. Barbara Dietrich and Joachim Perels (Frankfurt am Main: Suhrkamp, 1976), 241f.

29. Jahoda, Lazarsfeld, and Zeitel, *Marienthal*, 16.
30. Stijn Fens, "Celibaat, homohuwelijk, euthanasie: van de meeste katholieken mag de kerk wel wat progressiever," *Trouw*, January 27, 2022.
31. Eribon, *Returning*, 131.
32. Peter Mair, *Ruling the Void: The Hollowing of Western Democracy* (London: Verso, 2011).
33. Péter Csigó, *The Neopopular Bubble. Speculating on "the People" in Late Modern Democracy* (Budapest: Central European University Press, 2017).
34. See Seymour Martin Lipset and Gary Marks, *It Didn't Happen Here: Why Socialism Failed in the United States* (New York: Norton, 2000).
35. Theda Skocpol, "Voice and Inequality: The Transformation of American Civic Democracy," *Perspectives on Politics* 2, no. 1 (March 2004): 3–20, 9.
36. Ibid., 10.
37. Theda Skocpol, "Advocates Without Members: The Recent Transformation of American Life," in *Civic Engagement in American Democracy*, ed. Skocpol and Morris P. Fiorina (Washington, DC: Brookings Institution Press, 1999), 461–509. See also Benjamin Y. Fong and Melissa Naschek, "NGOism: The Politics of the Third Sector," *Catalyst* 5, no. 1 (Spring 2021): 93–131.
38. Michel J. Crozier, Samuel Huntington, and Joji Watanuki, *The Crisis of Democracy: Report on the Governability of Democracies to the Trilateral Commission* (New York: New York University Press, 1975), 164.
39. Thomas Ferguson, *The Golden Rule: The Investment Theory of Party Competition and the Logic of Money-Driven Political Systems* (Chicago: University of Chicago Press, 1995), 84.
40. Marcel Gauchet, *L'avènement de la démocratie* (Paris: Gallimard, 2016), 77.
41. James Heartfield, "The Failure of the Capitalist Class and the Retreat from Production," *Platypus Review* 70 (2014).

42. Timothy Snyder, *On Tyranny: Twenty Lessons from the Twentieth Century* (New York: Penguin, 2017); Jason Stanley, *How Fascism Works: The Politics of Us and Them* (New York: Random House, 2018).
43. Timothy Snyder, "The American Abyss," *New York Times*, January 9, 2021.
44. Paul Mason, *How to Stop Fascism: History, Ideology, Resistance* (New York: Penguin, 2022); Sarah Kendzior, *Hiding in Plain Sight: The Invention of Donald Trump and the Erosion of America* (New York: Flatiron Books, 2020); Madeleine Albright, *Fascism: A Warning* (New York: Harper Collins, 2019).
45. Putnam, *Bowling*, 21.
46. Shanker Satyanath, Nico Voigtländer, and Hans-Joachim Voth, "Bowling for Fascism: Social Capital and the Rise of the Nazi Party," *Journal of Political Economy* 125, no. 2 (April 2017): 478–526.
47. Andrés Rodriguez-Pose, Neil Lee, and Cornelius Lipp, "Golfing with Trump: Social Capital, Decline, Inequality, and The Rise of Populism in the US," *Cambridge Journal of Regions, Economy and Society* 14 (2021): 457–81.
48. Alberto Toscano, *Late Fascism: Race, Capitalism and the Politics of Crisis* (London: Verso Books, 2023).
49. Gabriel Winant, "We Live in a Society," *n+1*, December 12, 2020.
50. Ibid.
51. Christopher Cadelago and Olivia Olander, "Biden Calls Trump's Philosophy 'Semi-Fascism,'" *Politico*, August 25, 2022.
52. Dylan Riley, "What Is Trump?" *New Left Review* II, no. 114 (November–December 2018): 5–31; Corey Robin, "Trump and the Trapped Country," *New Yorker*, March 13, 2021.
53. Riley, "What Is Trump?," 6.
54. Heinrich Geiselberger, "Liquider Autoritarismus," *Philosophie-Magazin*, January 18, 2021.
55. Karl Marx, "The Eighteenth Brumaire of Louis Bonaparte," in *Surveys from Exile: Political Writings*, trans. Ben Fowkes (London: Verso, 2010 [1852]), 1:239.

56. Wendy Brown, “Apocalyptic Populism,” *Eurozine*, August 30, 2017.
57. Corey Robin, “The Gonzo Constitutionalism of the American Right,” *New York Review of Books*, October 21, 2020.
58. Ibid. For a restatement of this argument following Trump’s reelection in 2024, see Corey Robin, “President Trump Will Not Be as Powerful as He Seems,” *Jacobin*, December 23, 2024.
59. Adam Tooze, *Shutdown: How Covid Shook the World’s Economy* (New York: Penguin, 2021), 32.
60. David Broder, *Mussolini’s Grandchildren: Fascism in Contemporary Italy* (London: Pluto, 2023), 13.
61. Tariq Ali, “Adieu Boris, Adieu,” *Sidecar*, July 12, 2022, newleftreview.org.
62. R. W. Johnson, “Electability: Letter,” *London Review of Books* 37, no. 19 (October 7, 2015).
63. César Rendueles, “From Global Regression to Post-Capitalist Counter-Movements,” in *The Great Regression*, ed. Heinrich Geiselberger (London: Polity, 2017), 150.
64. Friedrich Engels, “Trades Unions,” *The Labour Standard*, May 20, 1881.
65. Paul Heidemann, “Behind the Republican Party Crack-Up,” *Catalyst* 5, no. 2 (September 9, 2021): 45–101, 48.
66. Cited in ibid., 70.
67. Tim Barker, “Dealignment,” *Sidecar*, November 11, 2024, newleftreview.org.

3. The Antipolitical Decade

1. Clément Solym, “Houellebecq opte pour l’iPad, manquant de force dans les bras,” *ActuaLitté: Les univers du livre*, December 31, 2010.
2. Stéphane Hessel, *Time for Outrage*, trans. Marion Duvert (New York: Hachette, 2011), 11–12.
3. Thierry Leclère, “Résistons à l’indifférence avec Stéphane Hessel,” *Télérama*, November 27, 2010.

4. Michel Houellebecq, *Submission*, trans. Lorin Stein (New York: Farrar, Strauss and Giroux, 2015), 37–8.
5. György Konrád, "Geistige Macht und Staatsmacht, Politik und Antipolitik," in *Antipolitik: Mitteleuropäische Meditationen* (Frankfurt am Main: Suhrkamp, 1984), 211.
6. "Macht des Wortes: Auszug aus der Rede Vaclav Havels auf der Helsinki-Bürgerversammlung in Prag am 19. Oktober," *die tageszeitung*, October 22, 1990.
7. Jan-Werner Müller, *What Is Populism?* (Philadelphia: University of Pennsylvania Press, 2016), 41.
8. Michael Stabenow, "Anlaufstelle für Merkel und Sarkoz," *Frankfurter Allgemeine Zeitung*, April 10, 2010.
9. Cristóbal Rovira Kaltwasser, Paul Taggart, Paulina Ochoa Espejo, and Pierre Ostiguy, "Populism: An Overview of the Concept and the State of the Art," in *The Oxford Handbook of Populism*, ed. Kaltwasser et al. (Oxford: Oxford University Press, 2017), 1–24, 9.
10. "How Populist Are You?," *Guardian*, November 21, 2018.
11. Gáspár Miklós Tamás, "The Mystery of 'Populism' Finally Unveiled," *Open Democracy*, February 24, 2017.
12. Jacques de Saint Victor, *Les antipolitiques* (Paris: Grasset, 2014), 3–4.
13. Philip Cunliffe, Alex Hochuli, and George Hoare, *The End of the End of History* (Londen: Zer0 Books, 2020), 57.
14. Nils C. Kumkar, *The Tea Party, Occupy Wall Street, and the Great Recession* (New York: Palgrave MacMillan, 2018), 63.
15. Ibid., 64.
16. Ibid., 74, 77.
17. David Graeber, "You're Creating a Vision of the Sort of Society You Want to Have in Miniature," interviewed by Ezra Klein, *Washington Post* blog, October 3, 2011.
18. Ibid.
19. Slavoj Žižek, "Occupy Wall Street: What Is to Be Done Next?," *Guardian*, April 24, 2012.

20. Slavoj Žižek, "Don't Fall in Love with Yourselves," in *Occupy! Scenes from Occupied America*, ed. *n+1* (London: Verso, 2011), 66–9, 67.
21. Stathis Kouvelakis, "Syriza's Electoral Quagmire Reflects Its Crushing of Greeks' Hopes," *Jacobin*, June 9, 2023.
22. Ekaitz Cancela and Pedro M. Rey-Araújo, "Lessons of the Podemos Experiment," *New Left Review* II, no. 138 (November–December 2022): 1–21
23. Amedeo Varriale, "Institutionalized Populism: The 'Strange Case' of the Italian Five Star Movement," European Center for Populism Studies, June 8, 2021; available at populismstudies.org.
24. For a comparison of the organizational structures of M5S and the Lega, see Elena Dal Zotto, "Populism in Italy: The Case of the Five Star Movement," PhD diss. (Libera Università Internazionale degli Studi Sociali, 2019); available at cidob.org.
25. Jessica Garland, "Labour's 'Three-Quid Voters': The Challenges and Opportunities of Opening up the Party," LSE Blog, January 20, 2016; available at blogs.lse.ac.uk.
26. Monica Poletti, Tim Bale, and Paul Webb, "Explaining the Pro-Corbyn Surge in Labour's Membership," LSE Blog, November 16, 2016; available at blogs.lse.ac.uk.
27. Kumkar, *Tea Party*, 21.
28. For a similar assessment, see Chantal Mouffe, *Towards a Green Democratic Revolution: Left Populism and the Power of Affects* (London: Verso, 2022).
29. Michel Houellebecq, "Donald Trump Is a Good President," trans. John Cullen, *Harper's*, January 2019, 49–51.
30. See the references in Kumar, *Tea Party*, 241.
31. Theda Skocpol, "Who Owns the GOP?," *Dissent* 63, no. 2 (February 3, 2016): 142–8, 146; in this review essay, Skocpol draws on her study, coauthored with Vanessa Williamson, *The Tea Party and the Remaking of Republican Conservatism* (Oxford: Oxford University Press, 2016).